Rodie Enj

C000090431

A MESSAGE FROM JESSIE

The Incredible True Story of Murder
and Miracles in the Heartland

BUCK BLODGETT

STORY MERCHANT BOOKS
LOS ANGELES
2015

STORY MERCHANT BOOKS

A Message from Jessie

Facebook: The LOVE>hate Project
Website: www.ligth.org
YouTube: The Love is Greater than hate Project

Story Merchant Books
400 S. Burnside Ave. #11B
Los Angeles, CA 90036
http://www.storymerchant.com/books.html

ISBN-13: 978-0-9963689-7-1

Editor: Lisa Cerasoli
Interior Design: Lisa Cerasoli & Danielle Canfield

Cover: Charles Hallett
Facebook: Charles Hallett Photo & Video

Butterfly Cover Art: Kathy Morton Stanion
KathyMortonStanion.faso.com
etsy.com/shop/KathyMortonStanion

For Jessie, the Light of my life.
For Joy, the Love of my life.

"I don't mean to offend your religious beliefs or speak as if I have any closer connection to God than you do, and you can call me crazy, but I'm not crazy. And if your religious beliefs can't harbor that a murderer could be forgiven, then they don't fully grasp Unconditional Love.

But that's OK. None of us can fully grasp Unconditional Love. I think we'll understand it much better when we're done here, like Jess does now."

—Buck Blodgett
A Message from Jessie

A Message from Jessie

BUCK BLODGETT

ACKNOWLEDGEMENTS

Jessie—you taught me to be myself, to give everything I can give, to fight for what I believe in, to defend the victimized, to be silly, to fully engage, and to believe in miracles.

Joy—you let me share my crazy signs with the world, pursue a new life purpose, write into the night for months, screw up, change my worldview and spiritual beliefs, and be joyful when it didn't make sense.

Family (Mom, Dad, Fred, Dana, Becky)—you were there when I needed you most.

Friends (Mark, Dave, Hans)—our lifelong bonds mean everything to me.

Remaining Family and Friends—you helped get me through. I love you all.

Jessie's Friends—you accepted her for who she was. You supported us in our darkest hour. We will always love you for both.

Clinic Family—you saw my worst days and lifted me up through them.

LOVE>hate Board and Team—you dreamed with me, and worked to make it happen. You are all great-hearts.

Hartford Police Department—you solved Jessie's case and answered our questions, you prevented future killings, you called us every day, kept your promises, and worked tirelessly.

District Attorney's Office—you were Jessie's voice, you fought for justice for her and my family, and you treated us like family.

Hartford Community—you buried Joy and me in a tidal wave of love for months. You donated to Jessie's Memorial Fund, ensuring a permanent music scholarship in her name at CMS and startup funding for her legacy project.

Beth Hermann, and Laurie Sullivan—you created the banner and wristbands that coined the phrase LOVE>hate and birthed our project.

Lisa Cerasoli—you taught this rookie author the ropes, showed me that less is more, worked with my schedule, and saw the weak spots in the manuscript that needed to be clarified, cleaned up, or canned. You understood the essence of this story from day one, never pulled me off course, always perfected the storytelling.

And finally, to my Creator—if we were capable of fully understanding, all the words of this book could be reduced to just two: Thank You.

SPECIAL THANKS TO THE FOLLOWING BUSINESSES

WTKM: for playing Jessie's song "Butterflies" on the airwaves, and interviewing me about Jess and The LOVE>hate Project.

USBank, Scoop deVille, Perc Place, Hahn's True Value, Schubert Theatre, Hartford Music Center, Mineshaft, Design Originals, Hanks, MJ's Market, Central Middle School, Hartford Union High School, Snap Fitness, And County Market: for putting out donation displays for months and helping support Jessie's Memorial Fund.

INTRODUCTION

This is a book about pain and Love.

There are people in this world that will feel the intense sting of deep, old wounds when they read this book. It is my wish for every single one of them, including the perpetrator, to subsequently experience a washing away of that pain by the greatest power in this universe: Love.

At the top of that list is Dan's family, especially his mom and dad. They are good people. They were kind and supportive to Jess. They unquestionably provided a loving, caring, quality home environment for their children. They had nothing to do with the choices their son made. And they have been through a hell that few can imagine.

I want them to know that I never intended to write a book. But I was led by my Higher Power to shine the brightest light in the darkest places, because the truth sets us free. All of us.

Also on that list is my wife. Joy cried every single day that first year, and almost every day since. But a week after Jessie was stolen from her she went back to work. We were taught in chiropractic school "To Give, To Serve, To Love," and that's exactly what she did, despite the indescribable pain and the giant hole in her heart. Much of Jessie's amazing strength and big heart came from her mom, who loved her more than anything in this world. Although her primary purpose in life—being a mom—is now gone, she continues on. I love you, honey.

Also on the list are Jessie and Dan's family and friends, who will relive this nightmare in their own private ways, when memories are stirred. And there are others...

I hope you, too, upon closing this book, understand the purpose of it all was Love.

I need to mention that I did not take notes during the trial, as I did with the butterfly stories and the other "signs." Nor did I request transcripts. I wrote this book from my memories of the trial. There may be some minor inaccuracies regarding sequence of events, DNA statistics, and such. Also, the conversations are not direct quotes; rather, they are recreations of the basic content and unfolding of events, as I remember them. In general, the book is a fair and accurate, but certainly not an exact representation of the trial. The events I call signs are real and true.

The following understanding permeated all my being in the wake of Jessie's murder. I didn't distinguish it at first, I just WAS it. I now believe it came from a Higher Place, and was given to me. It is the foundation for this book and the driving force behind my new life purpose:

An act of such incomprehensible indifference to human suffering and the sanctity of life MUST be answered with an even more incomprehensible Forgiveness and reverence for life.

LOVE>hate

A Message from Jessie

THE PHONE CALL

"And if we ever stop living this life oh so suddenly…"
—Jessie Blodgett/Ian Nytes, "Letter to Humanity"

HOLLY BURST THROUGH THE DOOR before she finished knocking. "Dr. Buck. Joy's on the phone. Something's happened. You have to pick up *now!*"

It was 12:50 p.m., Monday, July 15, 2013. I was in my office meeting with Lisa, the nutraceutical rep from NEI, after morning patients. Calm by nature, my alert level was slow to rise. I wondered for an instant why Holly had walked right in without waiting for a reply. She never did that. I watched Lisa look from Holly, to me, and back to Holly again. Lisa's body recoiled as she rose quickly and retreated backward out the door. My eyes returned to Holly, and now I saw the grave concern written on her ashen face.

Time was slowing down as I reached for the phone.

"Honey?"

Joy was crying, almost wailing. "Honey, it's Jessie. It's Jessie!"

"What honey?"

"I was just home a few minutes, for lunch. I heard one of her little piano students knocking at the door with his dad. I called up to her…I thought she must still be asleep. She didn't answer." Joy was talking fast now through the tears. "I went up to her room. I was mad that she wasn't answering, wasn't ready for her lesson…. She was in her bed. She wasn't moving as I talked to her. I rolled her over." Joy went on, sobbing. "She…she…she was blue, she was cold…there was a mark on her neck, bruising, blood speckles…and there were red dots in her eyes. I couldn't find a pulse."

"Honey, is she…?"

"Her femoral region was still warm…that gave me hope…I called 911. The dispatcher asked me if Jessie was responding to my CPR. I told her 'no,' and she told me to put her on the hard floor and try again."

"Honey, is she…?"

"The EMTs are here now. They just took over for me, and I called you right away. They just shocked her."

"Is she responding?!"

"No."

Joy was sobbing so deeply, I could almost feel her body convulsing in my chest. "Honey, is she…is she…?" I couldn't say the word. "…Is she…gone?"

Joy let out a moan from deep inside, but no more words came with it.

I packed up quickly and headed up the long hallway toward the front desk. The concern from the staff was palpable. Kim, our billing rep and my friend for ten years now, stopped me at the end of the corridor.

She took my hand, smiled, and tried to reassure me. "Everything's going to be okay," she said. But then she looked deep into my eyes and asked, "Right?"

I managed a small nod.

They say the eyes are the window to the soul. I saw myself in Kim's eyes on Monday, July 15, 2013. I saw her soul reacting to mine. It was then that the gravity of the situation fully registered. But I had also gone into fight or flight mode. Reflexively, I was mentally preparing to save my daughter.

The problem was there was nothing I could do. It was a thirty-one-minute drive home. I was thirty-one minutes from Jess, from Joy, and from the paramedics who were shocking my sweetie and pleading for her heart to restart. All I could do was this: pray. All I had was a plea to the God whose existence Jess and I had denied. Somewhere in the depths of my being I had always sensed He was there when I stopped analyzing and reasoning. But earlier this year, Jess and I had declared ourselves atheists.

Time stopped altogether on that drive home. I talked to God. I tried to listen. I begged Him to spare Jessie, and I held onto hope. I stayed positive. Joy had not said Jess was gone. She hadn't said anything.

The cars on the freeway were moving in slow motion. I could hear the sounds of their engines and tires. I felt the warm sun on my cheek. Beautiful puffy white clouds filled the bright blue sky. Two songbirds chased a large red-tailed hawk away from their nest. A black cloud of diesel exhaust belched out of the eighteen-wheeler ahead of me. I soaked in the whole scene, while talking to my business partner, Mike, who called to lend support.

There is an old Samurai saying I suddenly understood: *In the midst of battle the warrior hears the bird.* I was in a heightened state of hyper-awareness, intensely alive, feeling everything. Shock, disbelief, and pain magnified beyond words were juxtaposed against the simple timeless beauty of a sunny summer day in Wisconsin.

chapter two

WARD OF THE STATE

"Then when you die, it's with open eyes."
—Jessie Blodgett/Ian Nytes, "Letter To Humanity"

I EXITED THE FREEWAY ONTO Highway 60W toward Hartford. Primal instinct had taken over. I felt like a wolf returning to defend the pack, fearing he was too late and all was lost. My stomach knotted.

I turned right on Wayside Drive. As I rounded the corner and passed the tall berm full of cedars we planted when we moved in fourteen years back, the flashing red and blue lights came into view. Our long driveway was full from top to bottom with Hartford P.D. squad cars, Washington County Sheriff's Department vehicles, an ambulance, a fire truck, and unmarked detective vehicles. More law enforcement and first responder cars were parked on the road. I pulled up and parked behind them, unable to maneuver into my own driveway.

I got out and started up the long slope. Jeff was at the top, waiting for me. He was our neighbor, and a local pastor, one of three who worked with the Hartford Police Department. Today his kind face was not his own; it was borrowed for the occasion, like Holly's, like Kim's, worn with shock and despair.

I wanted only to get inside, to see Jess, to see Joy. But I stopped for the silent handshake and hug with Jeff, because I knew that on this day, and every day after, nothing was more important than the sacred connection between people.

Behind Pastor Jeff, a large boxy vehicle was parked. (It looked like a landscaping business truck, one that might have lawnmowers and shovels inside, except on the outside of this vehicle printed in block letters were the words: Crime Scene Unit.)

I went into the house. It was bustling with activity. Everyone was on task. EMTs were coming and going. Three detectives were huddled in the kitchen. I didn't recognize anyone; they didn't know me either. But when I passed them, their heads turned, their faces changed, our eyes met, and some lost their train of thought. Their reaction was something I would get used to in the coming months.

Joy was in the living room. A police officer in full uniform and a younger female paramedic, Shari, sat on either side of Joy. When Jessie was pronounced dead, before I arrived home, it was Shari who held Joy's hand, looked her in the eyes, and said, "I'm here with you."

When I entered the room and my eyes met my soul mate's, my life partner who bore Jess, I knew the truth: all hope was gone, and Jess was gone with it.

The tears streamed down Joy's cheeks, then mine. We held each other long and gently. There in our living room, in our darkest hour, all eyes were trained on us during our most private pain.

After Joy and I had hugged and cried for a minute or two, I said I wanted to see Jess. Silence. Eyes darted about, searching for a leader. Someone said Detective Thickens would be down shortly to speak with me. I didn't want to speak with him; we could do that later. I wanted to see Jess, touch her, hold her, talk to her, tell her I loved her more than anything in this world. I wanted to tell her I was sorry that I wasn't there when she needed help. I wanted to say goodbye. My chest constricted. My palms began to sweat. My breathing turned fast and shallow. I could feel my own heart beating.

Detective Thickens came quickly. He was a well-built middle-aged bald man with intelligence and sensitivity in his eyes. No one should have the job of telling a father that he cannot see his fallen daughter.

He began to explain, "Jessie is now a ward of the State of Wisconsin. It is the State's and my duty to protect her now, to ensure that her case is handled properly, and that justice is done for her.

"Her bedroom is a crime scene now. It's taped off and no one is allowed in. Not even you. I'm sorry. We must do a thorough and rigorous investigation, for Jessie. We'll let you see her when we're done."

The police and detectives were in Jessie's room until about 4:00 p.m. It seemed like a lifetime. Joy and I sat together on the couch in the living room all day, waiting. My heart ached to see Jess, to hold her. We were interviewed on and off throughout the afternoon.

As Detective Thickens questioned us, my mind flashed through old TV case documentaries we've all seen, where the family was the prime suspect. I felt a surge of anger at the thought that someone might suggest I could harm my angel girl, my most precious thing in this whole world. But that fear never materialized.

7

Not once throughout the course of the investigation did Det. Thickens, Chief Groves, or anyone in the Hartford P.D. approach me, or Joy, with anything but sensitivity, respect, and professionalism. Thickens asked all the questions that day. Some were hard ones to both ask and answer, but I understood he was doing his job. He had to protect and solve Jessie's case and bring her justice.

The word came down from upstairs that they were finished. They had taken all their photos and video, dusted for prints, examined every item in her room, and documented all of it. Finally, I could see Jess.

The portable ambulance bed was carried downstairs by five or six EMTs and officers. She was wheeled into our dining room, covered by sheets from neck to toe. But they were peeled back around her blue, lifeless face so I could say goodbye. After an eternity of waiting and absorbing the shock, my moment with her had come.

I was instructed not to touch her. She was evidence. My girl was evidence. I moved close to her side, crowding between all the EMTs and detectives. Everyone was staring at me. There was no light in her blank, open, fixed eyes. I couldn't hold her hand. I couldn't hold her tight and whisper that I loved her. I just wanted to lift her off the gurney, hug her long and hard, and talk to her. But they wouldn't let me. And they were all right there, crowded together, in our private space.

And then my moment with her was over.

They wheeled her out and loaded her into the ambulance, and I never really got to be with her, alone, to say goodbye, to tell her I would remember her every day forever and never stop loving her.

I stared blankly down the driveway as all the vehicles pulled away. Just like that, everyone was gone. The air was still, the evening was quiet, and our house was empty. Nothing stirred anywhere, not even a bird. They had driven away with Jess. She was gone, and we were a family of two again. How things had changed since I left for work this morning, when Jess was sleeping peacefully in her bed.

Joy and I talked, cried, and hugged on the couch.

She said, "Honey, marriages fall apart when something like this happens. We're going to have to stick together."

We both knew she had spoken the truth. I saw in her face the fear of losing me as well as Jess. I assured her I would stick by her, and she assured me of the same.

United in our pain and loss, the following year would prove to be the closest and best of our twenty-nine years together.

But the emptiness echoed through the house.

We had called key family members earlier in the afternoon. They spread the word. Our closest family called to express their love and deep sorrow, but no one else phoned. No one stopped by. The magnitude of what had happened began to sink in; this was no normal passing. Even our own families were giving us a day of space to deal, to absorb. This was so shocking that no one knew what to do. The loneliness was almost crushing.

Out our picture window to the west, pink and orange pastel streaks were all that remained in the sky as the sun disappeared below the tree line. Darkness was descending on Hartford. How could we face the night? Each silent, empty, agonizing second felt the length of

9

a lifetime. There would be no sleep. I felt like all of my being was screaming on the inside, unheard by an indifferent and unaware world.

And then the silhouettes appeared down by the road, slowly filing toward and up our long driveway. Jessie's friends. They didn't know or care what the right or wrong thing to do was; they only knew they loved her, and their shock and pain was unbearable too. Some heard that something was wrong, but didn't know she was gone, or couldn't believe it. Word spread on Facebook like wildfire. They came to find out, to be together, to support each other, and to be there for Joy and me.

They came in small groups. I met them at the top of the drive-way. First to arrive were Davis and Ian, from her inner circle at school. Then came Scott, Caleb, and Jessica, her camping and nature buddies. Then Jackie, Amelia, and Jacqueline, more best friends. Then Kelly and Cody, also the best of friends with Jess and fellow cast members from *Fiddler on the Roof*. And Moriah, from years of choir and musicals—she came up the drive too. Soon our house was full of twenty or thirty devastated amazing young people, now bonded forever with us by horror and love.

In the weeks and months to come, a tidal wave of love, support, and prayers rained down upon us from our community and beyond. But it was Jessie's friends, along with Joy, who got me through the first two days.

They stayed late, but Joy could not spend the night in our house, in our bedroom, twenty feet from where the bright, talented, nine-teen-year-old center of our universe drew her final breath. What happened was still a mystery to us, still in the beginnings of an active investigation.

But we were forming ideas. The marks Joy had observed on Jessie's neck and wrists were speaking to our imaginations. The detectives asked about her mental state. How dare anyone think our joyful young woman, so richly overflowing with purpose and life, might take her own? They were only considering all possibilities, as every proper investigation required.

But we knew otherwise. Someone had harmed her. Someone entered our home on a Monday morning, while she was sleeping and most vulnerable, and done the unspeakable. Someone had watched the light in her eyes flicker out, stealing her from us forever.

BUTTERFLIES

"I get this feeling I love that makes me want to cry...."
—Jessie Blodgett, "Butterflies"

JOY AND I SPENT A long and sleepless night a few blocks away, staring at the ceiling of a second-floor suite at the AmericInn. Each minute was like an hour as we speculated, ached together, wondered out loud what our Jess had suffered through, how long it had lasted, how much it hurt, how terrified she must have been. Who did it, and why?

We shared memories from her short life. But mostly we cried, holding each other. With the quiet came the images, and I became Jess. I felt her terror, felt every cell cry for oxygen as I gasped for air. I felt my consciousness waning, and all hope with it. I felt the panic growing as I stared into the face of my attacker and realized he would not grant the mercy I begged for.

The images would visit every day and night for months to come. Years.

We returned home with the morning light. The house was empty again. As the sun rose in the pale blue morning sky, we drifted from shock to grief to anger and back again. I became restless.

"Honey, let's go for a walk. I'm suffocating." No sleep and little food for twenty-four hours. I didn't want any. I was running on adrenaline. Our world had stopped. Nothing mattered but Jess.

Joy didn't want to walk. She was afraid that we wouldn't make it around the neighborhood without being swamped by support, or worse—questions she wasn't ready to answer. We agreed to just go down the driveway, get outside, and breathe the free air.

We walked slowly hand in hand down the driveway. At the bottom, we heard Peggy. With long brown hair flying, our kind next-door neighbor jogged toward us. Peggy had the "borrowed for the occasion" look on her face too. She had resisted the urge to come to our house yesterday and this morning wanting to respect the process and our privacy. But when she saw us outside, she had to come running.

The three of us discussed the events that transpired from yesterday until now, talked about Jessie, and wondered what might have happened. We hugged and cried and laughed a little and remembered my girl at the bottom of our driveway, about twenty feet from the road.

As we talked, a big, beautiful monarch butterfly flew out of Peggy's yard, passing about ten feet behind Peggy and Joy. It was not bouncing with the wind the way butterflies usually do but rather it was flying in a slow straight line, between the house and us, across our whole front yard, right in front of me.

As it was disappearing into the trees, my focus shifted back toward Joy and Peggy. Then, out of the corner of my eye, it stopped. It hovered in place for a few seconds, not moving at all but for the flapping of wings, then retraced its flight back across our yard in another slow and perfect line, until it passed by us again and back into Peggy's yard. The butterfly proceeded to fly back and forth ten feet from us, slowly, almost deliberately, retracing this exact flight path over and over again for several minutes.

Because Joy and Peggy were facing me, and the butterfly was right behind them, I was the one looking at it. Peggy caught me staring at it, and she turned to see it, too. Then Joy did the same.

Peggy then turned back, and with a subtle smile said, "That's Jessie."

I paused at the remark, and we resumed our conversation. Almost on cue, the butterfly flew off, bouncing haphazardly now in the breeze the way butterflies typically do. The butterfly flew so straight and slow and deliberately, and then, as soon as Peggy said "that's Jessie," off it went, carefree in the wind, and disappeared.

I realized I was attaching meaning to something that had none. I reminded myself that I was experiencing a fresh emotional trauma, and told myself I was looking for something that wasn't there.

I don't ever want to believe in anything just because I need to, out of desperation to make sense of something that doesn't. I've always valued critical thinking and reason over belief, religion, and superstition.

So I forgot about the butterfly.

Late that night in the hotel, with sleep not possible for two nights now—alone with my thoughts as Joy tried to rest, alone again with the images and the horror of what Jessie might have gone through in her final moments—I got up. I went into another room in the suite and closed the door. I went to talk to God.

Looking back, that was a strange thing for me to do. I was a self-professed atheist. Jess and I had watched some very compelling atheism videos in 2013, and wished aloud that believers would watch them with an open mind. Somewhere deep inside I have always sensed the Divine, especially when alone in nature, or in times of trouble, but never did I seem to find it in church, or with people who talked about God so doggedly.

As I sat in that dark hotel suite at three o'clock in the morning, mind screaming, I dropped my face into my hands, and spoke these words silently in my head: "If You are really there, if You do exist, I need to know. I'm breaking here, and I need to know, and I'm gonna need more than one sign this time, because I'm older and wiser and more cynical, and I've witnessed a lot of BS and lies...."

Only one other time in my life did I ask for a sign. That was nearly twenty years ago. The unbelievable response I had gotten to that silly request floored me, but I had let that memory drift off into the past, forgotten. Until now.

This time, the reply came before my face hit my hands. I felt a deep and powerful *something* that I've never been able to adequately describe wash gently through me. It went into my head, or through my heart, or both; it's hard to know. And with it came these words: *You already had the sign. I knew you'd be asking.*

And I remembered the butterfly.

A flood of memories filled my mind, and I vaulted back in time to the eighth grade talent show—maybe my proudest moment as her dad. Her coming out party as a musician, when she sang the very first song she ever wrote and brought the house down. Through the years, the song meant little to her but everything to me.

15

Jess had been too shy to play the piano and sing her song in front of her mom and me; she only worked on it when Joy and I were out. She performed it publicly, and for us, for the first time in front of the packed Central Middle School auditorium. That night in eighth grade, I saw that Jess was talented and gifted, and serious about music.

Sitting there alone in the dark, with my head in my hands and heartbreak pulsing through my body, my thoughts traveled forward from the eighth grade musical. I remembered times in the years that followed when I would inexplicably envision myself at Jessie's funeral with this song playing in the background. I'd see myself brokenhearted, proudly making sure everyone in attendance knew the music playing was Jessie's first song, written and performed by her. These were sporadic but recurring visions I had always dismissed as typical parental fears, not premonitions. I would consciously steer my thoughts from those dark places, putting the funeral scenes out of mind. Every parent worries about losing their child, right? Every parent probably has thoughts like that sometimes, right?

The name of Jessie's first song performed in breakout fashion to Dad's great amazement?

"Butterflies."

Two months after Jessie's death, while mulching leaves on a beautiful autumn day in the Heartland, it dawned on me that the monarch butterfly in our yard on July 16, 2013 was the only one I'd seen all summer. In fifty-three years as a nature lover, I can't recall seeing a butterfly behave that way. In fourteen years of living in this house and working in the yard, this was the only summer I saw but one butterfly. All the other years, I've seen hundreds.

16

chapter four

THE VIGIL

"I'll be there...I'll be there for you."
—Jessie Blodgett/Ian Nytes, "Letter To Humanity"

PEGGY WAS THE FIRST PERSON Joy and I saw on Day Two. Bless her giant heart. She broke the emptiness, gave us someone to talk to, and added some hope to the black and desperate morning after. But, around noon, our house began to fill with people again.

My older brother, Dana, drove up from Milwaukee. My mom and sister—from the Milwaukee suburb of Wauwatosa where we all grew up—aborted their summer vacation in Maine to make the twenty-four-hour drive home. My oldest brother, Fred, who they were visiting in Maine, hopped on a plane. So did Dad, from his summer home, which was in Maine too.

Mark, a non-blood brother, a friend since kindergarten, came. Our home phone, my cell, and Joy's cell started ringing and wouldn't stop. As the day rolled on, Jessie's friends returned. By late afternoon, the house was full with twenty friends, family, and neighbors. An hour later, there were thirty.

Chris, Joy's good friend, beat the rush, showing up with a mop and bucket to scrub our floors on knees still healing from surgery. She knew company would be coming, and Joy needed help preparing. Becky (my sister), did our laundry. Dana mowed the lawn. It was huge, but he didn't mind; he loved the riding mower. Casseroles, fruit plates, cheese and sausage and cracker trays, and a host of other dishes appeared from neighbors and strangers alike.

Phone calls were made for us, to get the word out, so Joy and I didn't have to. Chief Groves called from the Hartford P.D., as he would for sixteen days straight, including Sundays, to tell us to "hang in there." He assured us as new information surfaced Joy and I would be the first to know.

"All resources available to the Department will be for Jessie and your family until this case is solved," he said.

By evening, our home was full of people who loved Jessie. Cast members from the Hartford Players production *Fiddler on the Roof*, who Jess called her second family, debated whether to perform the second weekend shows without her. Jess was the Fiddler.

They ultimately decided, correctly, that Jessie would insist the show go on. And so it did. They invited our extended family that weekend to witness the most moving tribute to a fallen comrade I have ever seen. Although they had a second Fiddler available, they did not replace Jess, but rather put a candle in her place on the roof, leaving Jessie's violin parts to remain silent. They said she could not be replaced, so why even try.

Two or three dozen of her friends from Hartford Union High School, West Bend, UWM and beyond, including her inner circle of ten very close friends, eventually took over our living room. They embraced and cried and laughed and shared stories like only young people can, with innocent and open hearts. They weren't old enough to have seen death so close yet. Their grief seemed somehow different than the adults; maybe more shock and disbelief, and less utter devastation.

Josh was there. He called me "Dad" and Joy "Mom." Jessie was his first love. They dated for several months sophomore year, and although she broke his heart, Josh remained her loyal friend. Big, rugged, wrestling, football-playing Nick broke *my* heart when he knocked on our door, head down, and whispered that Jess was the first person he ever said "I love you" to. Then he said he'd be sure to invite me to his wedding one day, because I would never walk a daughter down the aisle now. Nick was Jessie's boyfriend for part of junior year.

And Dan was there too. He sat next to Jess as first violin for four years of orchestra, her very first boyfriend freshman year of high school.

I tried to hug and thank every one of her friends. They were precious to me now in a way I couldn't have imagined forty-eight hours earlier. They were my lifelines to my lost girl. I loved every one of them for themselves, and for their love for Jess.

At one point in the evening, Joy asked me if I had heard about Dan.

"No, what?"

"He was called into the Slinger Police Department by the Washington County Sheriff's Office," she said. "He said something about the police misidentifying his blue van in connection with an attack on a woman in a park three days earlier in Richfield. I reassured him and said that the police would be interviewing all of Jessie's friends, that it was just routine. I tried to tell him not to worry, but he seemed a bit shaken."

Dan was family now, like all of Jessie's friends. He would need support and love on these darkest of days like so many who were so young and innocent.

A while later, an almost blood-curdling wail broke out in our front yard. It penetrated our brick walls and I felt it in my gut. Apparently, another friend had arrived and learned of the unthinkable news. Or so I thought.

Joy hurried down the stairs, petitioning the group to go outside and comfort the girl in our front yard.

It wasn't until months later that I'd learn the wailing young woman in our yard was crying not for our Jess, but for her boyfriend—Dan.

GOODBYE, SWEETIE

"I get this feeling I can't explain..."

—Jessie Blodgett, "Music"

EVERY DAY THAT FIRST WEEK our home filled with more people. After driving twenty-four hours nonstop from Maine, Mom, who was eighty-three, and my sister, Becky, would then come up daily, making the trip from Wauwatosa to Hartford. They'd stay all day, every day, just like my brother, Dana.

Joy's entire family arrived—parents, two sisters, two brothers, and all their spouses and children. They were Jessie's "Canada family." My brother Fred and my dad flew in and stayed for two weeks. Jessie's friends returned daily, as did my best friends, Mark and Hans. Hans had bagged his family vacation in Minnesota and returned home immediately upon hearing the news. After four nights in the local hotel, the first three without sleep, the bustle and chaos of bonding and sharing such devastating heartbreak was shifting the energy in our house.

Jessie's friends and cousins took turns visiting her bedroom.... They spent time alone there, and time together. They made peace with her, and her loss. They played the video games she used to play with them when they were kids. At times, we even heard the familiar laughter of teenagers rumble out of her room.

The outpouring of love and devotion to her blessed our home. From a distance, this could have looked like a weeklong party—our house overflowing with people bonded by death, and celebrating her life.

Joy decided after four nights that she could sleep in the house again. Thank God. The hotel bill was mounting, and I had begun to wonder if we would ever move back home. No more staring at the ceiling at the AmericInn. No more long middle of the night strolls through the empty streets of Hartford.

Jessie's good friend, Davis, virtually lived at our house that first week. He and Fred worked feverishly to prepare for Jessie's service on Saturday. Davis, our resident computer genius, recovered photos from friends' computers and phones. Her best girlfriends, Jackie and Jacquelyn, assembled a life history—nineteen years of images on four large photo boards provided by Shimon Funeral Home. Moriah arranged for the Hartford Union High School choir to perform. Ian, Amelia, Kelly, Cody, Aaron (Ian and Jackie's younger brother) among others all helped every day, all week. It was a collective labor of love and despair, organized by Fred, but everyone contributed.

Those early days are burned forever into my heart. So much pain. So much loss. Jacquelyn barely stopped crying; I don't know how she managed the photo boards. Jacquelyn was a brilliant artist. A week earlier she had drawn a temporary tattoo on Jessie's tummy of a puffy dandelion blowing away in the wind. She kept sobbing and saying it was the last time she would ever touch Jess.

It was heart wrenching to watch. We all supported her, and each other. It was the best of humanity rising to overcome the worst of it.

Joy and I leaned into the grieving process and onto the broad shoulders of so many who loved us. We vowed to face every aspect of this with open eyes and raw, but unbreakable hearts, in honor of Jess. She would have told us to feel it all, live it all, accept it all.

Jess was a young woman with an indomitable spirit. She was the girl who ran out into traffic on Highway 60 near Pike Lake to rescue a turtle that wasn't going to make it across the road. She was the girl whose purse came from Ecuador, because it was a Fair Trade item, and even a stranger from halfway around the world deserved a chance to build a life.

The way to meet this horrible tragedy was not with anger and bitterness. She would never allow evil or selfishness to suck her down to its level. We had to respond to this incomprehensible act with the best of our true selves, not the worst. To honor Jess.

On Wednesday, the County Medical Examiner released her body back to Shimon Funeral Home. Everyone at Shimon treated Joy and me with great sensitivity and professionalism. They asked the questions no parent ever wants to answer: "Burial or cremation?" "What would you like to do with the ashes?" "What color vase?"

They prepared her body for us to see on Thursday. She was to be driven to the crematorium in West Bend later that day, and this was my final chance to be with her alone. Mom, Becky, Fred, and I spent a few minutes together with her in an empty room at the funeral home. Then they left. Finally, it was Jess and me.

I held her hand. It was so cold, stiff, and lifeless—it startled me. But I held it anyway and talked to her. I told her how much I loved her. I told her she brought me more joy than I could say. I told her how much I admired her fierce and constant defense of animals and the downtrodden.

"Sweetie, I am so proud of how you lived. Every part of me will always love and remember you forever. I wasn't there when you needed me to protect you. I'm sorry."

And then she whispered on my heart: *It's OK, Dad. You will always be my hero.*

Joy could not imagine her Jess burning. It was me who convinced Joy that Jess would want to have her ashes spread at Pike Lake and in Maine, rather than be buried in the frozen Wisconsin earth.

But I was second-guessing myself. I had to stay with Joy. It was a hard day, and she needed me, but I was sending my daughter away to be incinerated and not even going with her. What kind of dad was I?

Fred, my mom, and Becky accompanied Jess to West Bend that day, where she was cremated. Fred would not let her go into the furnace alone.

Day Six. It was the twentieth of July. Saturday morning dawned clear and sunny in Hartford. When we moved here in October of 1997, Hartford was a rural farm town of eight thousand. You could often smell manure from the surrounding farmlands when the winds and the seasons were right. It was only a half-hour drive from Milwaukee, but it seemed like a different world.

I didn't want to move to Hartford. But Joy was offered a position at a new clinic, Hartford Chiropractic. The owner required his doctors live in the community they practiced in. I reluctantly agreed; we needed her income. We had opened Blodgett Family Chiropractic outside of Milwaukee six months earlier, and our new clinic wasn't generating enough yet.

My roots, my family, my lifelong friends, and my clinic, with all the staff and patients I loved, were in the Milwaukee area. I wasn't invested in Hartford. But when Jess left us my eyes opened. I let in the overwhelming support of this community, and I saw the heart of this town. I now love Hartford, and never want to leave.

Hartford has grown dramatically. Fourteen thousand people live here now. We have the ten million dollar Rec Center, an exceptional school system that Jess thrived in, and the Schauer Arts Center—a jewel of a theatre drawing performers that you wouldn't expect to find in farmland USA.

Its essence is still that of an idyllic small town environment. It's quiet, friendly, and safe—the perfect place to raise a family. There were two murders in Hartford in the past century.

Until Jessie's made it three.

Shimon Funeral Home had a 250-person capacity, according to the fire marshal's code. Over 400 people were packed into Jessie's service that sunny Saturday morning. A line three-to-four wide snaked out of the breakout lobby, down a long corridor, out the west door, along the whole width of the building, around the corner and down the whole length of the building, into the parking lot, and down the street.

Over 1,000 people had come to remember Jessie from Hartford, Milwaukee, West Bend, all over Southeast Wisconsin, and as far away as Maine and Alberta, Canada. Most of them never even got inside.

Joy and I spent hours hugging people and receiving condolences. Every person who came was important to us, whether we knew them or not. "Butterflies" played softly in the background, as it had in my premonitions. Every friend, every family member, every stranger was sacred now. They were all hearing Jessie's music, seeing her photos, remembering, and loving her. And so we loved them back.

An hour after the scheduled start time, Funeral Director Steve Shimon found us outside with hundreds of people who had yet to be greeted. He let us know that we could not delay any longer. Pastor Ben began his eulogy. Joy and I sat on a couch in the front of the room in a haze, guests of honor at our only daughter's funeral.

We held hands and listened to Pastor Ben quote the Bible and talk about our daughter's life, and Heaven. I could feel Joy's angst when he spoke of God's Plan. She had often wondered out loud how people could think that God planned for a sick f*** to enter our home, bind our innocent girl, terrorize her, brutalize her…. What kind of a God could plan, or even allow, that?

And then my time came.

Normally self-conscious in front of a large crowd, I walked slowly to the front, asking God for composure, so I could get out what I had to say to honor Jess and everyone who had come.

Since the butterfly event and the middle-of-the-night plea, I had begun to talk to God again. It wasn't that I *believed* in Him now; it was that I *felt* Him. A great peace and calm came over me. Slowly, deliberately, my eyes surveyed the room, wanting to connect with every soul present.

Twenty or thirty seconds passed. They must have thought I couldn't speak. Faces were drawn, crying, haggard with the weight of a promising young life snuffed out before its time, and from having to watch a dad deal with it. I felt the white-hot energy of collective compassion pour out to me. I scrolled all the way from the far left to the far right side of the room. One lone face was beaming. It was my brother, Dana.

How could I explain to others, or even understand myself, the Great OKness, deep Peace, and profound Love I was experiencing so shortly after my angel's murder? It made no sense. I was at her funeral for God's sake, but it was beautiful and one lone face in that room sensed it and mirrored its joy: Dana.

I began....

"There is no possible way for me to put into words what you have all meant to Joy and me...the community, the Police, Jessie's friends, and our families.

"Jessie was...

My shining star,
My close, close friend,
My best teacher,
My biggest fan,
My social and environmental conscience.

"This is a devastating blow, but her strength and spirit is in me too, and will not be defeated.

"I love you my little sweetie, my beautiful, proud young woman.

"Love will always be stronger than hate."

I had no clue at the time what those words were about to become.

THE ATTACK IN THE PARK

"How could we ever see the beauty
That it could be?"
—Jessie Blodgett/Ian Nytes-"Letter to Humanity"

TWO DAYS EARLIER, THURSDAY MORNING on the eighteenth of July, Joy and I went to the Police station to visit Det. Thickens. After the initial questioning on Monday at our house, he had returned Tuesday and Wednesday with follow up questions and information. This time, before the usual crowd descended on our home in the early afternoon, we thought we'd pay him a visit. Mornings alone in the empty, silent house were pure pain. I looked for any excuse to get out.

Detective Thickens welcomed us into his office. Later on we learned that he and his force worked eighteen-hour days for sixteen days straight on this case. But he made time for us.

We chatted about the developing case. He began with a question about Jessie's first boyfriend, Dan. This struck me. He started with questions about Dan yesterday and the day before, too. Joy and I told him Dan was a good kid. He had been a friend of Jessie's since ninth grade, and he was welcome in our home. We had no suspicions of Dan, or any of Jessie's friends.

We discussed several possible suspects, everyone we could think of. We hated even considering names, knowing we were discussing innocent people, but we owed Jessie justice and our community protection from whoever was capable of this.

But when Thickens asked about Dan again, I said, "That's the third straight day you've opened with a question about Dan. What's up with that?"

"Just asking," he replied.

After two hours, Det. Thickens left the room. But another officer had come in minutes earlier, whispered to him, and then stayed.

In the awkward silence after Det. Thickens left, I asked the other officer, "Why did Detective Thickens ask us about Dan again?"

"Didn't we tell you about Dan yet?"

"No, what?"

"He's under arrest."

"What?"

"He's been in the Washington County jail since Tuesday, when the Slinger P.D. called him at your home and asked him to come in and help them answer some questions."

"No way." I looked at Joy. She was as wide-eyed as me.

"He was initially questioned regarding a knife attack on a woman in Richfield County Park Friday morning. She allegedly fought him off, wrestled the knife from him, and he fled. She called police, described his vehicle, and also described him for a police sketch artist. The Sheriff's Dept. matched his vehicle to her description from their database. They had logged his license plate at that park two weeks earlier doing routine patrols. He admitted being there."

"Oh my God…." I had never heard of such an attack in Rich-field, a nearby town much smaller than Hartford. Added to the fact there had been two murders in Hartford in the one hundred years prior to Jessie's, it was too stunning a coincidence.

Our minds raced. Dan? A knife attack in Richfield, his hometown? The same park he had taken Jess to two weeks earlier? The park she then excitedly showed me, proclaiming she had found a new place for us to go foraging for wild edibles?

Questions came to mind fast and furiously. Who was this heroic young woman who fought off a knife-wielding attacker twice her size, and had the presence of mind to describe both him and his vehicle? How did police connect the dots? And what if the park incident had been on a different day? Did the weekend delay investi-gating? If so, did the delay cost Jess her life? They called Dan in for questioning about the attack in the park just a day after Jess was attacked.

I put that last question out of my mind. These officers were proving with every passing hour how much they cared, how hard they were working on this, and how well trained they were. This was their community, their watch. They took this personally. They would not rest, literally, until Washington County was safe and justice was done. To cast any shadow of blame on them was wrong of me. I tried to wrench my mind out of the "what ifs."

chapter seven

THE CHIEF SPEAKS

"These thoughts in my head,
All I want is to put them to bed...."
—Jessie Blodgett/Ian Nytes, "Love by Proxy"

DAY THIRTEEN. HARTFORD POLICE CHIEF David Groves called, as he had done every day since the fifteenth of July. Today was different though.

"How are you holding up? How's Joy? Hang in there." He began every call this way.

"We've finished our investigation. We're ready to go public," the Chief said. "But before we do, we want to tell you and Joy everything."

The Chief promised all along we would be the first to know anything new. He kept his promise. He was calling to set up a visit to review the criminal complaint with us before he announced it to the world.

The Chief, Hartford P.D, Joy, and I had remained silent about ongoing developments in the case. He briefed us daily on whatever information he could, but mostly he had to say things like, "We are gathering new evidence and learning new things daily," and "We're getting close." His face showed how badly he wanted to tell us what he knew. He was a father too. But he couldn't.

We understood. The urge to share with our loved ones what little we knew was irresistible. But the integrity of the investigation was paramount. No one wanted to solve this case only to see the killer go free because of a mistake.

The Chief endured pressure from the media, the community, and local alderpersons. For two weeks they clamored to release what he knew. Local officials wanted information so they could respond to the public's fears. The media wanted a story.

Media descended upon our house and neighborhood for days. News vehicles would park on our street and shoot footage of our home—the home where the teen actress died mysteriously.

Reporters from the four major news networks in Milwaukee, and even a *Dateline* NBC Correspondent from Chicago, walked up our drive, knocked on our door, and offered condolences.

"Sorry, we can't talk about the case," I'd say.

"I understand, but how do you feel about the Police Chief's refusal to share information?" they'd inquire.

"Well, I'm grateful. He calls me every day, even Sundays. He tells me that despite the pressure he's under he'll answer only to Jessie. He promises daily to do whatever it takes to solve her case, and his *only* priorities are; Jessie, number one; and my family, number two. He says when it's time to release information, Joy and I will be the first to know. I love and respect him for that."

None of this made the Ten O'clock News, of course.

They wanted anger. They wanted controversy. They wanted a villain, a drama, someone to blame. I wanted to honor Jess. She wouldn't have gone there, and neither did I.

Day Fifteen.

Joy heard the knock on the door. It was Chief Groves and Detective Thickens.

My stomach turned as the four of us moved into the living room and sat down. I feared for Joy, for what she was about to hear. But I wanted to know every last detail. I wanted the clearest picture of what my baby girl, my strong and beautiful young woman, Jess, had suffered through. The least I could do for her was try to fully understand what happened. It sounds crazy, but if I could experience what she did, maybe it would ease some guilt. Or maybe I could somehow take her pain and carry it for her. I had been up on her bed a few times, holding my breath longer than I ever have, seeing what it felt like. I owed it to her to go through what she was put through. It made no rational sense, but it was valid to a mourning dad. Of course, I could never understand what she must've gone through, nor could I ever carry it for her.

Joy wanted to know everything too. The Chief's instinct was to protect her (both of us really) from the graphic, dark details. We made it clear to him to not hold back. We had the right to know. We had the need to know.

They say the truth will set you free. I believe that. I know that. We must shine the brightest light into the darkest places of our souls.

Only the light can heal such blackness. There is sickness and evil in this world. We can't hate it. And we can't hide it, deny it, bury it and turn away, pretend it's not there, like a child who closes their eyes at night so they can't see the Boogeyman. We must shine Light into it. And so we must know the whole truth, face it, embrace it, and expose it to the light of day.

The Chief began. He read the report in its entirety. Many parts we already knew. There was no forced entry; Dan had let himself in our unlocked side door. It happened sometime around 10:00 a.m. A neighbor had seen a van in our driveway. There was nothing missing or out of place. The killer wasn't there to steal anything. It appeared to police that he went directly to Jessie's room. There were no signs of struggle—apparently he surprised her in her sleep. She never had a chance.

Then the chief got to the parts we didn't know. He told us of a cereal box found in the trash at Woodlawn Park, where Dan was caught on video camera that Monday morning. The box had been identified by Dan's parents as the same kind of cereal commonly found in their home. A matching one had been found in his van.

Inside the box were several ligatures, one with apparent bloodstains on it. Also in the box was a unique type of ventilation tape, Intertape 698. A roll of that was found under Jessie's bed. Another roll was found at the scene of the knife attack in the park three days before Jess was killed. And more was found in Dan's home. On the tape was some human hair. DNA testing would later confirm that it was Jessie's.

The report continued. The coroner found ligature marks on Jessie's ankles, as well as the ones on her wrists and neck we already

34

knew about. She had been hog-tied. A gag ball was found in the box as well.

Now my body reacted. Piloerector muscles in the skin on my arms tingled and made my arm hair stand up. I turned immediately to Joy. She was crying. Images were filling both our minds. Every new detail was a new image, a new piece of the puzzle of the last moments of our girl's life.

Who could do this to her? And why?

The Chief continued. The report spoke of Dan's lies to police and to his parents about a job he said he was at that Monday morning—a job the police confirmed he never had. He had pretended to work there for months. The report discussed his computer, now in custody, which showed a history of searches for serial killers and their methods. It showed searches for the definition of spree killing, two or more killings in multiple locations within three days of each other. We didn't miss the fact that the attacks in the park and our home were three days apart.

The report also spoke of a novel Dan was writing, which contained many eerie parallels to Jessie's murder.

We would have to wait for lab results. But the State Crime Lab would move testing for this case to the front of their line. Those results would later confirm that Dan's DNA was on both ends of the rope that the county medical examiner had matched to the marks on Jessie's neck. Jessie's DNA was in the middle of that rope. We had the murder weapon, and DNA from both the killer and the victim, and no one else's was on it.

BREAKING NEWS

"Anything can happen to you,
Anything can happen...overnight."
—Jessie Blodgett, "Overnight"

THE HALF-HOUR INTERVIEW WAS over. Charles Benson of TMJ4 was in our living room packing up with his cameraman. It was the second of three news interviews we did at our home on August 1, 2013, the day after the first court appearance, two and a half weeks after Jessie was taken from us, and shortly after the press conference with Chief Groves.

It was odd and surreal to have known news personalities in our home. I wished they were there for some other reason, like we won the lottery, or they discovered dinosaur bones under our house.

I hit it off with Charles Benson. Of all the reporters who had been trying to interview us, Benson showed the most humanity. Starting with small talk, I found out he was a triathlete, and a good one. Being an ex-ultramarathoner myself (sadly sub-average, but game), I wanted to hear his story. He was training hard for the Madison Iron Man, a qualifier for the Super Bowl of triathlons—*The Iron Man*, in Hawaii. He lived by the philosophy strong mind, strong body, strong spirit.

On the way toward the door, Charles turned and said, "What are those?"

He was looking at the four photo boards that were displayed at Jessie's funeral.

Then Benson said, "Let's take five more minutes, you and I will hold each end of a board, I'll point to a photo, you tell us about it, and we'll film it."

So we did that.

Again, he and the cameraman were packed and leaving. At the door now, he inexplicably turned again. His eye had been drawn to two plastic butterflies someone glued to one of the photo boards. They must have heard my butterfly story. I hadn't even noticed they were there.

Benson walked back into our living room. "Wait…what are those? Is there any significance to that?"

I had told the butterfly story many times over the past couple weeks to the point where I was tiring of it and thought others must be too. I thought maybe I had turned it into more than what it was…just a butterfly flying around. When Charles asked that question, I thought—*Don't make me tell this on TV….*

The indescribable feeling washed through me again, and something in my heart spoke softly to my head. *"It's OK, people want to know. Tell the story."*

That night the butterfly story was heard by thousands throughout greater Milwaukee on the Six and Ten O'clock News. I couldn't help but notice that Benson almost left twice. It felt as if the story itself insisted on being told.

A WALK IN THE WOODS

"Cuz you can't define
Something of the heart
And not of the mind…"
—Jessie Blodgett, "Music"

SEVERAL DAYS LATER, I GROUP-TEXTED fifteen or so of Jessie's friends, inviting them on a "remembering Jessie walk" on the trails of Pike Lake State Park, where she and I often hiked. I needed to be with her friends again. I felt closer to her when they were around. Alone time offered no distraction from the overwhelming and constant aching. The only cure, and a temporary one at that, was connecting with others.

A random group formed, about a dozen of us, including our next-door neighbors, Jason and Peggy.

Not all of Jessie's friends knew each other at the onset of the hike. It was a sunny and beautiful summer day, and we had a nice time in nature, remembering her, sharing the pain, laughing, and just spending time.

Ben was quiet. He didn't really know anyone there. He was from West Bend, not in the Hartford Union High School group of friends. Jess met him through a local social justice and environmental activist group. Ben was a talented writer, a bright and empathetic young man. Jess looked up to him. She had a lot of exceptional friends. She attracted and pursued quality people.

Ben spent a lot of time at our house the week after her murder. And he gave an eloquent speech about how much he had admired Jess at her funeral. We grew close, and so I asked him to join us on the trails.

At some point in the hike, someone mentioned the butterfly story. I told it again for those who hadn't heard, adding the story about the TMJ4 interview this time. People asked questions and added their own comments and stories. Ben was silent except when he asked, "What kind of butterfly was it?"

On the drive home, with just the two of us in the minivan, he said, "I have to tell you something."

He was at work, on the organic farm, in the days after Jessie's murder, when he noticed a large monarch butterfly flying toward him. It landed on a tall stalk of grass close by. He has always been an animal and nature lover, and he approached the butterfly, closer and closer, seeing how close he could get, until, at eye level, he was a foot away.

"The thought just came to me. This is Jessie," he said.

Ben found himself silently asking the butterfly several questions, the big questions, for about two minutes, while it perched on the tall stalk of grass a foot from his nose. It never flew away.

I asked Ben if he had ever been so close to a butterfly for so long. He said no. I asked him if the butterfly talked back.

"Sort of," he said sheepishly.

"What did it say?"

He told me he *felt* the butterfly say, "You are asking the wrong questions."

I asked what he thought that meant. He felt he was being told that the answers he was seeking are too big. Specific questions are too limiting to allow for the fullness of the truth about the nature of life and reality.

Which, strangely enough, was a concept Jessie and I had recently discussed on one of our last nature walks.

DARIAN FINDS A SHELL

"So go ahead...
And look for answers...
That you'll never get."

—Jessie Blodgett, "Music"

AS THE WEEKS PASSED, THE gnawing ache worsened. The wound was deep and the loss immense; it couldn't be absorbed all at once. Joy and I talked openly and frequently about every aspect of Jessie's life and death, with others and in our quiet time alone: The fact she had been hog-tied and gagged. The strangulation by a friend who had obviously been planning and fantasizing about this for a long time. The possibility that she looked into his eyes as her hope faded, and he slowly squeezed the life out of her while she begged silently for mercy. The likelihood that she was sleeping when he started, so she awoke to the realization that he was binding her.

It must have seemed like a dream at first. What disbelief and terror she must have endured. And physical pain. What a monumental betrayal. What a colossal violation.

We both knew that we must go fully through the grieving process. We understood from day one that any feelings or thoughts that we buried or failed to confront would inevitably resurface to be dealt with later. We deliberately approached every day, every moment, with eyes and hearts as open as we could.

A bottomless sea of love, support, and prayers poured in from thousands of family, friends, acquaintances, and strangers. We let it in.

A select few who had lost children of their own were there to prepare us.

"It will come in waves."

"It will get worse for a long time."

"The pain will never go away. You'll just learn to survive with it, function each day with it."

But no one we knew had lost an *only* child. They all had children left to love. What were we going to do? We were parents without a child to love.

Steady my whole life, I felt bipolar now. Sometimes I was this guy: half my heart died with Jess, the remaining half was torn in two. And other times I was this guy: I have suffered the most unimaginable loss, yet I feel wrapped in the arms of a Divine Love stronger than any loss, and it is gently and gradually showing me the Great OKness, the amazing news that I didn't believe could really be true.

I had the growing awareness, not like a belief, but like just knowing and seeing, that there really was something out there, and It was there for me now, revealing Itself to me in Its perfect timing, in layers I could grasp, giving me some hope.

42

Ciji awaited me in treatment room four. She had been a patient for two years. She brought her colicky baby boy in for treatment, and her boyfriend too. I was breaking all the rules of practice that I had subscribed to over my whole career—never talk about yourself; ask questions about them; ask about their physical pain; ask about their lives. And I was about to break the rules again.

I had been talking about Jessie constantly since she passed. All my patients knew what happened. It was all over the news in Milwaukee. I learned early that almost everyone *wanted* to talk about her and about what happened.

I had always thought that I, as their doctor, needed to be "up" for patients. Now I was being real, showing honest emotions, having deeply personal conversations, hugging patients, staff, family, and friends alike, telling everyone I loved them. Dana now hugged me and said "I love you" every time we met. We never did that; it was amazing. The deeper connectedness with everyone in my life was getting me through the days.

I was hearing frequently how strong and inspirational I was. I wasn't trying to be strong. I just had a freedom to be myself. I didn't feel strong. I felt needy and devastated, but also purposeful and called, like I had a duty to Jess and to humanity to react to this in the highest way. Sometimes I felt strangely blessed. How could that be? My daughter, my best friend, was dead.

I always replied, "I'm not strong. Love is strong. I'm no different than anyone else. We all have it in us." A burning ember deep inside had been fanned to full flame, and now all it wanted was to spark the ember in others to full flame too, until all souls awakened and the sickness of the world was washed away.

Ciji told me she lost her cousin, who was also her best friend, seventeen years ago. I was hearing so many stories now. Never before this did I realize how much loss and grief so many people carried around.

People never talked to me about their lost loved ones or their encounters with sexual violence before. They did now. Why don't we talk about these things? I'm sure it was my fault; I wasn't someone who others perceived as a trustworthy confidant for these two issues before I lost Jess.

But it is also our culture's fault, too, especially our male culture, which discourages open and truthful sharing of sadness or trauma. Buck up. Deal. Get over it. Move on. Quit whining. We miss the opportunity to help each other and bond in more meaningful ways.

Looking for some comfort from Ciji, I asked, "I guess the pain eventually goes away, huh?"

Ciji didn't hesitate when she said, "No."

We finished our visit. I worked my way up to the front desk.

Chris, our Chiropractic Technician, said, "I have something for you."

She pulled a small, beautiful white seashell out of her scrubs pocket. Holding it up between her thumb and index finger, she turned it so we could see the inside. The inside was shinier, pearly with purple markings. Chris explained that her daughter Darian found the shell. When Darian showed it to her mom, Chris said, 'Oh, it's purple. That was Jessie's favorite color.' Darian, knowing Jessie's story, said, "Mom, give the shell to Dr. Buck."

As Chris handed the shell to me, I looked closer.

"No way." I whispered.

"What?" Chris asked.

The very distinct purple marking on the inner surface of the white shell was in the rough shape of a butterfly, complete with darker central body, two wings, and two antennae.

How is it that the shell of a living clam, underwater for years in a random lake in southeast Wisconsin, can bleach out to a beautiful white within, leaving a very distinctive purple marking that resembles a butterfly? How does that shell, after years, wash ashore and into the hands of the teenage daughter of a coworker? How does that teenager, who never knew Jess, then connect the dots and instruct her mom to deliver the shell to me at the only time in my life when butterflies have special significance and deeper meaning?

Am I starting to see things? Is it because of a very deep subconscious need? Or, is it because those things are really there, always have been there, part of an ultimate reality underlying an illusory physical world, and I am finally in a place where I am being given eyes to see? I had asked for a sign that He was real. I had said that I would need more than one.

Little did I know where this was headed....

chapter eleven

WELCOME TO FACEBOOK

"Why can't you see…
I'm singing this song for you?"
—Jessie Blodgett/Ian Nytes, "Letter To Humanity"

JESSIE PUT ME ON FACEBOOK in 2010. She thought it was time. I was not happy about it.

"Honey, I told you I don't want to be on Facebook. I don't have time for Facebook. My life is too full as it is. Now people are going to want to be *friends*, and I won't reply, and they'll think I'm blowing them off."

"Dad, calm down. Facebook is easy. You can be on it as much or as little as you like."

"No. I want to have real relationships and spend real time with people, not have superficial cyber friendships. Can you take me off now?"

"No."

"Honey! I told you—"

"Dad, Facebook is so cool. You will be so much more connected to so many more people."

"Yeah? How deeply?"

And on it went.

We debated my concern over the potential for our culture to devolve, to lose the ability to have meaningful social interaction due to time spent on the computer instead of face-to-face. She laughed at me, but in her loving way, where I felt respected for having a different opinion than hers, outdated as it was.

It took me just over a month, but I responded in writing, real manual handwriting, to every one of the thousand cards and letters that people sent to us after Jessie was murdered. Our community, and people beyond—from coast-to-coast, and as far north as Alaska—had flooded us with love and prayers.

Everyone deserved a response. Everyone deserved to know the difference they made. Everyone cared about Jess, and their words about her were all I had now. And when I was done, I, too, knew it was time. Something inside me said so. I think it was her.

So, I got on Facebook. It was September of 2013, three years after she had created my profile.

Jess was right. A whole new world opened up. I reconnected with old friends. I made new friends. And, imagine this: I started spending more real time with people and having more genuine conversations than ever before.

I became a regular at our local coffee house, the Perc Place, home of the world's best wall graffiti: *Unattended Children Will Be Given an Espresso and a Free Puppy!* It was one of Jessie's favorite places. I became ten times more social than I've ever been. I started listening to music a lot more, and stopped watching sports on TV. I became more like her.

Every off day, or half day, I met with two or three people, just to talk, to share grief and develop friendships. It was beautiful. Every moment counted. Every word and opinion mattered. It was the only thing that soothed the pain. Facebook expanded my universe, just as she argued it would. I wished I had followed her urgings sooner. I wished I had visited with *her* at the Perc Place more.

But she was gone now, and all I could do was live full out every second of every day, in honor and memory of her, hoping beyond hope that she somehow knew, somehow was watching.

I imagined I felt her presence, and it seemed she was pleased.

Through all this socializing a central theme began to emerge and take shape. The seed of a higher work was germinating in our conversations. We talked of the power of Love. We talked of male on female violence, culture shift, mass awareness, shining Light into the darkest places of humanity. We dreamed of changing the world. Fueled by grief and loss, a project was being born.

I leave you to Facebook....

◼ Jessie Blodgett

July 12, 2013

Just got a job offer as a part-time choir director for a church! Ah, my life just keeps getting better and better.

◼ Jessie Blodgett

July 12, 2013

A Fiddler on the Roof! Sounds crazy, no? Finally, the time has come: After six weeks of hard work and dedication, it's time to perform the show for all of you! I hope to see you there. —Feeling jazzed at Schauer Arts & Activities Center.

◼ Jessie Blodgett

July 14, 2013

Never have I ever had such a good time at a cast party. Playing Never Have I Ever...with Kelly Krill and 6 others.

◼ Buck and Joy Blodgett > Jessie Blodgett

July 16, 2013

Dear Family and Friends, Monday morning, July 15th, our sweet beautiful angel Jessie left us. This is an unthinkable loss for all of us who knew her, who loved her so much, and who she loved so much. There is a giant hole in our hearts that may never mend, but we will love each other more and better, because that's what she would have wanted. Jessie was a shining light, strong and principled. She cared about people, animals, nature, and social justice. She spoke out fiercely about male violence against women. We are immensely proud of her short life, of who she was, of what she did. Jessie, my baby girl, beautiful young woman, we love you, sweetie. Mom and Dad.

Kyle Martin

July 16, 2013 at 7:29 a.m.

We have lost one of the most self-less, beautiful and intelligent people I have ever met. For the short time I knew her, I could immediately see her talent, her kindness, her openness, her beauty and so much more. What a loss. My love to her and to family and friends who grieve.

Paul Hermann

July 16, 2013 at 8:43 a.m.

When I think of Jessie, I go back to seventh grade when she performed her own song at the Central talent show; it was inspirational and breathtaking. I will never forget the love and kindness Jessie passed abundantly to all people, and how she made my life better.

Friend

July 16, 2013 at 8:46 a.m.

Whenever I think of Jessie, I just think of this kind-hearted, smart, beautiful woman who never judged anyone. She has helped me through so many things....

Friend

July 16, 2013 at 9:11 a.m.

I think she spread more smiles and fought harder for her beliefs during her life than most people ever will.

Hannah Snyder

July 16, 2013 at 9:13 a.m.

I met Jessie six weeks ago during Fiddler on the Roof. Those six weeks will always live on in my memory as some of the happiest times I've ever had. Jessie was so sweet and loving to me and I will always remember her infectious smile. You raised an amazing person. She has accomplished so much during her short time on this earth and know that she is watching you from Heaven, where she can be the angel she truly is. I loved her so much and I will miss her terribly.

Teacher
July 16, 2013 at 1:21 p.m.

I've probably had 10-12,000 students in my career. Every once in a while one comes along who is really special. Jessie was really special.... Such potential.

Teacher
July 16, 2013 at 2:29 p.m.

...A small girl with a spirit the size of the Atlantic Ocean will transform people's souls in ways that are awesome and inspiring.

Emily Jaszewski
July 16, 2013

Lover, fighter, protector, friend. It is devastating to know that your beautiful soul has departed from this world. Your light was so bright and short-lived, but it illuminated everything and everyone you touched. Thank you for gracing us with your wisdom and many talents. It is only fitting that the legacy you leave is one of joy, hope for humanity, and a deep desire to create beauty. Rest in peace, my love. You will be sorely missed. I am proud to call you a friend.

Michael Patrick
July 16, 2013

Sometimes, if you are lucky, you meet a person who has so much crazy spirit that they unconsciously force you to improve your idea of what it means to be alive. They leave a trail of hope in all they do, simply by their nature. Jessie Blodgett gave me so much hope. Her intelligence, curiosity, fearlessness, and kindness were inspiring and unforgettable. For the immeasurable loss the world will suffer by her absence, I know myself and many will strive to be better people. RIP my friend, you will be so missed.

⬛ Ivan Röösli
July 17, 2013

Dear Jessie, I still remember you sitting by the piano, with so much soul and emotion, singing with all your heart...this is...how you shall be remembered, because it shows how you are on the inside, soulful and always nice to everyone, caring, loving, forgiving....

⬛ Erin Sullivan
July 20, 2013

How is it even possible to comprehend that something like this could happen—to you of all people? You were such a force of nature.... You were a beautiful person in every way. Open-minded, whip smart but thoughtful, strong-willed but compassionate, with a perpetually unique sense of humor. In ten years, I never stopped admiring your tenacity, your poise, and your complete fearlessness. Not to mention your natural musical talent. Singing, writing, playing the piano or the violin, teaching or performing; you could do it all. You were going to inspire and enlighten people. You were going to take the world by storm. I'll miss your Light, and the Light you would have brought to each and every person you would have met, if you'd had the chance. I feel thankful to have ever been lucky enough to know you, and call you my friend.

⬛ Buck Blodgett
August 20, 2013

Hi everyone. Forgive me for ignoring your friend requests for three years now. Jessie put me on FB against my will. Now, it's time.

Most of you know by now that we lost our beautiful, intelligent, musical, talented, big-hearted, sweet angel on the morning of July 15 to the violent outburst of a "friend." Jessie, I love and miss you beyond words, sweetie. My life will never be the same, but it will now be devoted to your cause. More on that later, friends and family. I love you all.

Jess, you are not only not forgotten, I feel you near me, sweetie. Hundreds, thousands, are hurting bad over your loss, all without the support Mom and I have. But LOVE IS STRONGER THAN hate and always will be. We will all honor your life and your death by becoming better people and making our communities closer and more humane. By calling out haters. By challenging ignorance. By showing our Love more. Watch us, sweetie.

Love, Dad.

🄵 Tyler Sandblom

July 17, 2014

Jessie, I just can't find words…. You were fearless, charming, and talented and you never failed to brighten my day. I will never forget the first time I heard you sing. I was in the band room and there were people crowding around listening to you as if they were watching a superstar take her stage. I won't ever forget when that superstar asked me to share that stage with her. You taught me more than anyone will know. You inspired me and challenged me and changed me in ways I needed. You touched my soul, and I hope you continue to guide people's souls up in Heaven. You are a superstar, and I am blessed to have known you.

This is what I lost. This is what the world lost.

LOVE > hate

---

*"Darkness cannot drive out darkness; only Light can do that.
Hate cannot drive out hate; only Love can do that."*
—Martin Luther King, Jr.

"HELLO?"

"Hi, is this Mr. Blodgett?"

"Yes, it is."

"Hi, Mr. Blodgett. This is Paul Stephens. I'm the Fire Chief here in Hartford. I'm not sure how you're going to feel about this, but our first responder, Shari Pfeifer, and I have been wondering what we can do to help your family. Shari was the woman who sat with Joy until you arrived home on July fifteenth."

"Okay, well, thanks, Paul, wow…. What are you thinking?"

"We had an idea that we would like to do a community candlelight walk to remember and honor Jessie, and to help everyone come together and heal. Would that be okay with you? We'll take care of all planning, everything. Don't you worry about a single thing, just enjoy it, if you can. Would this be a good thing for your family?"

I was blown away. We had received such an outpouring for a month now. How had I missed the goodness of the Hartford community? How had I lived here for sixteen years and not grown closer to these people?

A few weeks later, about five hundred people showed up at West Side Park in Hartford. There was a six-foot banner on the stone pavilion. Beth Hermann made it; her kids performed in the school concerts and musicals with Jess. The banner said: LOVE>hate. Unbeknownst to us, another friend, Laurie Sullivan, purchased hundreds of baby blue wristbands. Everybody was wearing them. They had "LOVE>hate" imprinted on them, along with an inset image of a butterfly.

There was a small table set up with photos of Jess, a ceramic monarch butterfly, and a beautiful poem called "Love Never Dies." The poem's last lines were: *"When all that's left of me is Love, give me away as best you can. I'll be home, waiting for you."*

A local band, The Minority, was setting up in the pavilion to perform their new tribute song, "For You, Jessie". The Hartford Union High School Choir would be singing, as well.

My stories about butterflies and words from the funeral were apparently making their way around. That night the "LOVE>hate" banner and wristbands appeared all over Facebook and YouTube, and then on all four evening news channels in Milwaukee. I couldn't believe how Jessie's story was spreading. Something was happening here.

We were all given candles to light and carry and we started off on our trek through downtown Hartford. The bike path wound through the woods to the Rec Center, where the people Jessie called her second family were waiting—the cast of *Fiddler on the Roof.* We gathered around the entrance as Jerry Becker, the director of the Hartford Players, gave a short speech about Jess. And then they sang.

Their haunting voices rose and fell. What is it about music that touches us at the core? And soft light in the darkness, too? When the singing ended, our shadowy cast of five hundred rolled quietly along toward the Mill Pond, with candles flickering in the inky night.

As we crossed the footbridge, a soft glow appeared in the distance. Nearing the pond, we saw hundreds of candles in paper bags floating on the glassy water. They swayed in peaceful rhythm with the easy motion of the pond. Some high school kids in a rowboat hustled to light the last bags before we arrived.

Paper lanterns lined our pathway for two miles, as did signs that said "Never Forget" and "LOVE>hate."

The Mayor escorted Joy and me along the route. When we arrived back at the starting point, our five hundred walkers and their flickering candles assembled in front of the pavilion. They sang sweetly along with the song rolling out of the speakers. *"…And maybe, just maybe…those butterflies will fly free…. Fly free…fly free…butterflies."* Hartford was singing Jessie's song.

Days later, I sat at my dining room table. Images rolled through my mind: the candlelight walk, butterflies, the "LOVE>hate" banner, the news coverage…. Profound thoughts and words about sickness and hate in the world, violence against women, and the power of Love—insights came to me effortlessly in creative bursts, streaming into my head. I sensed, again, that something was going on here. It felt like I was being sent messages, and I wrote them down.

There seemed to be a convergence of ideas, people, and events, all pointing to something new. It felt like I was in a canoe being borne down a powerful river and all I had to do was stay alert and paddle when the river called for it. Suddenly I realized a project was being born. And I was supposed to do something about it.

The LOVE>hate Project was to become an official organization with a clear mission. We would need people to help build it and run it. We would need a Facebook page. And we would need a website.

But I'm not a computer guy.

And websites cost money.

A day or two later, there was a knock at the door.

It was Ian, one of Jessie's closest high school friends. Ian and Jess used to debate and challenge each other. That was their thing, arguing points, both bursting with opinions on what was wrong with the world and what they needed to do about it. Ian would later say on *Dateline* that Jessie changed the way he thought. I'm sure that went both ways. They respected and loved each other.

Ian was just getting started in life. He lived on his own and worked full-time at Walmart from the day he finished high school.

"Hi, Buck. Can we talk?"

"Sure, come on in. Great to see you, Ian."

He ignored my handshake and pulled me in for a hug, like he always did since Jess died.

"You hungry?" I asked.

"Nah, not really. Thanks though."

"Come on, I know you can eat something...."

"Okay, whaddya got?"

We looked in the fridge and set him up.

"So what's up?" I said.

"Well, I've been thinking, kind of about my future. I really want to start my own web design business. I thought maybe I could build a website that was somehow dedicated to Jessie as a way for me to learn the ropes. Would that be okay with you?"

I smiled on the inside. This was not the first coincidence I'd witnessed since Jessie passed.

And it wouldn't be the last.

THE 8th HOLE

"It gives you this feeling you can't ignore."
—Jessie Blodgett, "Music"

IT WAS LATE AUGUST, FIVE weeks since the day our lives changed forever. Life had become a bittersweet ebb and flow, an ongoing tsunami of outward love washing over the private hell Joy and I always felt now. Sometimes it felt as if life was a bad dream that we might just wake up from. But tiny miracles fueled my hope in the midst of the emptiness and loss. I experienced a greater connectedness to family, friends, and even strangers now.

Especially with Dana.

My older brother and I loved each other, but we never spent much time together. By late August, it was time for me to at least try to resume some normal activities other than work. So we locked into playing eighteen holes of golf every Thursday. We talked about Jessie, shared memories and sorrows, talked about the case, ourselves, Dana's son Max, celebrated an occasional great shot, and enjoyed walking the course. Thursday became my favorite day. It was going to suck when the snow flew again and ended our golf year and our time together.

The eighth hole at Hartford Golf Club is a one-hundred-sixty-five-yard, par-three. (You might have to be a golfer to get this butterfly story, but hopefully not.) Dana was on the tee box taking a warm-up swing. I was pulling a club out of my golf bag, looking toward the green, when I saw a monarch coming at us from way down the fairway. It was flying slowly in a straight line again, just like the one in the driveway did, not the way butterflies usually fly. Closer and closer it came, in a beeline straight for us. When it reached us, it fluttered around Dana for several seconds, then around me for several more, and then off it went, haphazardly away, bouncing here and there in the wind, the way butterflies usually fly.

And now I'm feeling that feeling again, that profound OKness. I'm feeling blessed.

I tee up my ball and prepare to swing away. In the back of my mind, it occurs to me that I have never gotten a hole-in-one. Now, I'm expecting a miracle.

I connect poorly, off the toe of the clubface and push it twenty yards right of the pin into the greenside bunker. Oh well, so much for butterflies.

In the sand trap minutes later, I connect poorly again, hit it thin and nuke it over the green into the far left bunker. It rolls up the steep backside of the sand trap and stops on the uphill slope, defying gravity and leaving me with the dreaded downhill sand lie—I mean severe downhill. It looked like the ball shouldn't have been able to stay there without rolling back downhill. No way can I get this out of the sand in one. And if I hit the perfect shot and somehow get out in one, no way I can keep it on the green.

I enter the deep sand trap and climb the steep backside to my ball. This is the worst sand trap lie I ever remember having. I have a great round going—two over par—but it looks like this hole is about to blow up my score.

I take that awkward steep slope stance. This is an impossible shot—not to mention I suck out of the sand.

And then suddenly I remember the butterfly at the tee box, and that magical feeling comes, the perfect peace, the Great OKness. I'm going to make this shot; I just know it.

I'm aware of my own thoughts: *You're not going to make this shot. You've never made a shot like this. No one, not even Phil Mickelson, could make this shot. This is one in a million…*. The feeling defies logic, but in the moment, I think again: *This shot is going in.*

I open the clubface wider than I normally dare to and swing. The open face makes perfect soft contact. Sand flies everywhere, and the ball pops high in the air despite the impossible downhill lie. It covers the fifteen feet across the bunker and lands a foot past its lip. Then it one-hops onto the fringe and begins the slow trickle downhill. Forty feet, thirty feet, gaining speed, curving hard left to right, twenty feet…tracking…ten feet from the pin now…tracking…. Oh, my God, it's looking good…. It plunks softly and gently into the cup, center cut.

Dana erupts.

I put my head down and smile as tears pool in my eyes with another unexplainable confirmation.

chapter fourteen

TIMELY MEETINGS

"Take a chance, make a change, and start to live...."
—Jessie Blodgett/Ian Nytes, "Letter To Humanity"

AUTUMN DESCENDED ON WISCONSIN. I'VE always liked the changing of the seasons—the crisp night air and the spectacular fall colors. But the waning of daytime and the lengthening nights felt different this year. Trees shed their leaves, the rolling green landscapes browned and died back. Northern air delivered dropping temperatures, as always. But this year I felt the cold not only in my bones; I felt it in my heart. Life in Hartford was going dormant for the impending winter freeze. It felt like death.

I stayed busy. I was living moment to moment more than ever now, spending time with people, family, friends, and Joy. I no longer cared about many of the things that used to be important: financial goals, sports, how good the yard looked compared to the neighbor's yard. That stuff was trivial now. What I cared about now was connecting more meaningfully with every person I could, and trying to bring Love into a world that was looking increasingly superficial and selfish from my perspective.

I finally dropped in on Paul Stephens, the fire chief.

I had been meaning to pay him a visit ever since the candlelight walk on August 15, just to say thanks. The Fire Chief wasn't big on "thank yous," though. He moved right past that and on to a story he'd been meaning to tell me.

"The walk didn't feel like the right place to chat with you privately, Buck. Anyway.... So, I was sitting here in my office with Shari after you lost Jessie, when the candlelight walk idea came to us. I needed to get out of the office, get some fresh air, and think it over. So I went to Subway. I parked in the Hartford Library lot by the mill pond to relax and eat.

"I was thinking about my brother-in-law, the mayor, wondering if he would support such a thing to help the town heal. Well, who pulls up and parks right next to me? My brother-in-law, the mayor!

"He tells me he was thinking about something like this too. Sure, he'd support it. He would even attend and walk with us.

"We said our goodbyes. Then it occurred to me that we should have music, because Jessie loved music. Maybe the Hartford Players would sing. I didn't know any of them, but I knew Tony Anderek would. Maybe Tony could connect us. So, I finished my sub and made a mental note to call Tony later.

"Now I'm ready to head back to the station when I see someone walking up the bike path toward the Mill Pond. I kid you not—it's Tony Anderek. Tony says he wants to help. He promises to contact the Hartford Players, he's sure they'll do it. Then he says, 'Contact Moriah. She leads a group from the Hartford High School choir. I bet Moriah would get them together to perform at the walk too.'"

Paul continues, "Now I'm driving down West Sumner wondering how to find Moriah, as I've only met her once. I see a group of kids walking along the sidewalk. They're summer camp kids from the Rec Center. Who's their summer camp leader? No kidding—Moriah. She's leading the group."

No way says my brain as the Fire Chief tells his story. But my heart smiles again.

Paul continues, "I pulled over to chat with Moriah. She said she'd love to organize a choir group to perform at the walk.

"When I get back to work, all I can think about is the three chance meetings I just had over lunch, and how easily and quickly everything fell into place, as if it was meant to be."

Well, Chief, maybe it was.

GOETHE'S COUPLET

"Until one is committed, there is hesitancy, the chance to draw back. Concerning all acts of initiative (and creation), there is one elementary truth, the ignorance of which kills countless ideas and splendid plans: that the moment one definitely commits oneself, then Providence moves too. All sorts of things occur to help one that would never otherwise have occurred. A whole stream of events issues from the decision, raising in one's favor all manner of unforeseen incidents and meetings and material assistance, which no man could have dreamed would have come his way. Whatever you can do, or dream you can do, begin it. Boldness has genius, power, and magic in it."

—Goethe

I'VE LOVED THIS QUOTE FOR three decades, since first hearing it in a personal growth seminar in Seattle. I have experienced the truth of it. But never in all my years had I seen Providence moving like it was moving now. Coincidences, timely meetings, signs, fortuitous events, people thinking the same thing independently. Even the scientist in me was noting the growing body of data.

First it was the case:

Melissa Richards, when tackled from behind by a knife-wielding man nearly twice her weight, somehow fought him off, took the knife, and had the presence of mind to describe both him and his vehicle.

Detectives got the suspect to admit where he was the morning Jess died, thus leading them to the evidence.

The garbage bins at the park had been emptied just two hours before the evidence was stashed there—it sat there for three days waiting for police to find it. The garbage was picked up twice per week; another day and the evidence would have been gone.

Had any one of these things happened differently, we would have an unsolved case.

Then, there were the ongoing butterfly signs.

A few words at a funeral took on a life of their own, ending up on banners, wristbands, Facebook, YouTube, and the evening news.

Ian knocked on my door asking about web design.

The Fire Chief organized a five hundred-person event over a lunch break.

In the coming months, resources would begin to fall into my lap from out of nowhere. I would meet new people for coffee. Many would soon become Board Members and Presenters for our young project.

I would meet Bill, who had a Master's Degree in Nonprofit Science. (I had never heard of such a major.) He had experience helping people build nonprofits from the ground up, and helping them obtain funding. Bill traveled in Wisconsin philanthropy circles.

I would meet John, my friend and now pastor, who would embrace our project as if it were the second coming of Jesus. John would expand my understanding of what was happening here. He would also invite me to breakfast with Pat, a national expert in

66

educational consulting. Pat teaches people how to promote their expertise so that schools across the country hire them for presentations.

I would reconnect with Barbie, a childhood neighbor and friend who I hadn't seen for thirty years. Barbie worked with several local organizations like the Milwaukee Human Trafficking Task Force, Celebrate Recovery, and Exploit No More.

One of my patients, Anna, would return to the clinic after a year's absence, listen to my story, and offer to help. Anna is a graphic design artist. Now we had a social media expert to create weekly e-newsletters for our website and Facebook.

And on and on....

Over that first year, I felt that if there was something or someone that The LOVE>hate Project needed in order to take the next step toward success and making a difference, that resource would find its way to us. All I needed to do was be willing, keep listening to Providence, keep working at it, and continue to take risks to reach out daily.

But I've gotten ahead of myself....

Back to early September.

COURT

"You gotta…
Feel the love you felt before
You felt the hate that closed the door…"

—Jessie Blodgett, "Overnight"

AT THE FIRST COURT HEARING Joy and I ever attended, Dan was formally charged with first-degree intentional homicide for killing Jessie. That was in August. Now it was September 4, 2013. This was the second hearing, our second visit to the Washington County Courthouse.

How strange it was, like being in a movie. Joy and I, along with my mom, Dana, and Becky, sat together on the hard classic oak benches on the left side of the courtroom behind D.A. Mark Bensen, and Asst. D.A. Sandy Giernoth. A few of Jessie's friends sat behind us. On the right side of the courtroom, behind the defendant and his attorney, sat Dan's large extended family and his pastor.

The rear door to the courtroom opened. The murmur hushed as all eyes turned to the deputies escorting Dan to the Defense table. He wore wrist and ankle shackles and an orange jumpsuit. I felt like everyone expected me to be vengeful and angry at the sight of him. Instead, I was sad.

Dan showed no emotion. Others later expressed anger at his smirk. But it seemed to me the grin was just an awkward cover for his shame. I don't know. For whatever reason, I felt bad for him. I glanced across the room at his parents. Their faces showed worry lines and pain. I had seen those lines before…in the mirror. I wondered if Dan noticed that the four parents here were aging like the President.

At the first hearing back in August, we listened as Judge Martens reviewed the charges. The judge asked the defendant and his attorney a series of questions to establish that the charges were understood by all parties. Today, we hoped to hear Dan's plea. Would he tell the truth? Admit he did it? Plead guilty? End what would otherwise be a grueling and drawn out legal process right now? Or would he let it all play out, putting my wife, our family, and his own through months of agony and frustration?

Neither thing happened. Nothing happened.

No plea was entered at this hearing. Nothing substantial was accomplished at all, in the eyes of a layperson waiting for accountability and the truth. The hearing lasted less than ten minutes. Some minor formalities were performed. I don't even remember what they were; I was too busy being frustrated. Joy and I had both canceled patients for half the day, and others had taken off work as well. The judge and attorneys pulled out their calendars and picked the next earliest date available to schedule the next hearing.

We had waited all month for this next step, for the wheels of justice to begin turning. But we were learning how our legal system worked. Each step must be taken one at a time, so the judge has time to evaluate motions before ruling, and so the State and the Defense each have time to prepare and react. For the families, it was agonizing, assembling in court every four to eight weeks just to get one step closer to trial, to closure, where there are no winners, no matter what the outcome.

I dislike the word closure. Friends said, "When the trial comes at least you'll have closure."

Joy hated that word. What was closure? It was talked about as if it was some good thing. What was so good about it? Jessie would still be gone forever, her suffering would in no way have been alleviated, and we would be left to feel her profound loss forever. Alone.

Nonetheless, I looked forward to each court date. Every hearing moved us closer to the day when Jessie's voice could be heard again—when we no longer had to hold everything we knew inside. There was so little we could share for fear of compromising the case and prejudicing the community.

f Buck Blodgett

September 5, 2013

It was oddly like a wedding yesterday—you know, friends of the groom on one side, friends of the bride on the other—except it was the Washington County Courthouse. Groom's side was nearly full. What were they feeling and thinking? How much do they know? Were they there to defend their family member's innocence? Or just to stand by and support, because that's what families do? They know because they can talk. Who will talk for Jessie? Bride's side was pretty empty. Her voice is gone. So many questions screaming for answers. But we must be patient, you know, right time and place, to "protect the integrity of the case." Okay, Jessie, you will be silent and patient and strong, for as long as necessary. No problem. One day, right time and place, your voice will be heard again, loud and clear, impacting the world as you always strove to do, touching minds and hearts wherever possible, searching for truth, spreading love. And what of me? Who will nuzzle their cheek against mine and say, "Daddy, your beard leftovers are scratching me!" Where is the third car in the driveway when I come home from work? How do I stop Joy's daily tears? Why is our music room always silent now? And where are the kids, the daily parade of kids, coming to our house, coming to my daughter to be inspired and encouraged, to learn music and laugh?

Jess, your strength is in all those kids, and in Mom and me, and in everyone you touched, and your legacy will forever be LOVE>hate.

Missing you for now, sweetie.

SHANNON TAKES A TEST

"Next thing you know you will be able to fly...
All because you had the heart to try..."
—Jessie Blodgett, "Overnight"

IN MID-SEPTEMBER, A WEEK after the second court hearing, my phone rang. People were still calling a lot to check in, see how we were, and offer support. This time it was Hans. He was all revved up, as usual.

Hans, my running buddy—we've been bonded by blood, sweat, and tears. Literally. When I was burning out on running, my midlife passion, meeting Hans re-stoked my fire.

Hans came into my clinic years ago with a bad hip and a broken spirit. He credits me for saving his running life, but he did more for me than I did for him. I've never met anyone more enthusiastic about anything than Hans was about running.

He got me off the paved roads of marathons and onto the wood-land trails. He got me out of Nike's and into the invigorating muddy freedom of barefoot running. He broke me from the tedium of the same, endless miles, and turned me onto tempo runs, intervals, stride-outs, cross training, team racing, and ultra running.

Hans and I would go on three-hour-long runs on the trails of the Kettle Moraine State Forest. Every time it was a new trail, a new adventure into undiscovered territory. He would talk nonstop, dreaming of running with the fabled Tarahumara Indians in Mexico's Copper Canyons, or tracking down the White Ghost, the legendary Caballo Blanco.

Hans was in the process of delivering on his dreams. He became Facebook friends with Caballo Blanco and had loose plans to travel to the Copper Canyons when he got the news that the body of his hero had been found on a remote trail in the Rockies.

Hans planned to run across the Rockies and the Grand Canyon. He said one day we'd qualify for Badwater, the most badass race on the planet, where your shoes melt if you stray from the white center line on the road across Death Valley.

Hans expanded my vision. We loved each other like brothers. We motivated each other. Ultimately, we qualified for and ran the Boston Marathon together.

Four days after a twenty-miler in ninety-degree heat, Hans dropped at the finish line of The Cow Chip, a local 10K we were racing. He said he didn't feel right. I walked him toward the first aid tent, but before we made it, he sat down under a tree and had a massive heart attack.

He survived the widow-maker that day. The experience bonded us for life.

I answered my phone.

"Hey, I gotta tell you something," Hans said, all juiced up. "It's a big day. Shannon took her driver's test. She was really nervous. She told me that she learned from Jessie to take a second, look within, tell herself she can and will do it, and think positive."

Jess and Shannon were Facebook friends. They lived in different towns and went to different schools. They were two years apart. But their crazy running dads brought them together, as did Facebook.

"So, in the DMV before the test she asked Jessie for help. She was worried about parallel parking. As she sat behind the wheel, about to start the test, she took a second, thought of Jess, and thought positive.

"When she looked over her shoulder to back up, there was a beautiful monarch butterfly fluttering around the rear windshield. She was in a parking lot in the city of Waukesha, nowhere near a field or flowers. She told me it seemed out of place, a strange coincidence. She said it was a sign from Jessie, and she knew she'd do fine."

She did. Shannon passed her test and got her license.

Another small branch sprouted on my growing tree of spirituality.

PARENTS OF MURDERED CHILDREN

"Feeling sorry for yourself
Won't get you nowhere."
—Jessie Blodgett, "Overnight"

AFTER THE SECOND HEARING, I took a drive up to the Courthouse at District Attorney Mark Bensen's request. When I arrived, I was escorted to the conference room. Mark, Assistant D.A., Sandy Giernoth, Detective Rich Thickens and Chief Groves were waiting. They wanted to talk about our new LOVE>hate Project. They wanted to strongly advise me to remain silent until after the trial. Their advice was critically important, but I resisted.

I felt that Jessie's killer had not only made her suffer, and stolen her life and her voice, but was now silencing mine. He was taking away the only thing I had to keep me sane: purpose. I had to speak for Jessie and make her life matter. I had to forward her legacy project and turn this unthinkable tragedy into something good. They were telling me I couldn't. I was frustrated, angry, and depressed.

But I knew they were right.

After our meeting, Ali, the Victim/Witness Program Coordinator, asked me if I contacted Parents of Murdered Children yet. POMC was a support group she recommended. She was trying to hold me over until I could come out with The Project.

I said, "No." We had so much support from family and friends I hadn't felt the need to call POMC.

But the shock was wearing off, and people were calling and visiting less, and I was ready to talk with others who had suffered a similar loss. Her question was timely.

She walked me out of the D.A.'s office and handed me the Parents of Murdered Children handbook, which she had given me back in July too.

I had thrown that one out.

I thanked Ali and left. Reaching for my car keys while exiting the courthouse, I looked at the pamphlet in my hand for the first time. The image dominating the cover of the Parents of Murdered Children handbook was a great big monarch butterfly.

I felt the weight lift from my head and shoulders. My frustration, anger, and depression dissolved, replaced by the Great OKness. I couldn't help but chuckle. I had thrown this butterfly away once, yet it found its way back into my hand at a time when I was hurting so badly.

Time rolled on.

f Buck Blodgett
September 29, 2013

Facebook's asking "what's on your mind?" Always you, sweetie....

chapter nineteen

HOW DEEP IS MOM'S LOVE

"If we haven't got,
Then we should give."
—Jessie Blodgett/Ian Nytes, "Letter to Humanity"

OCTOBER 10, 2013. NO SIGNS for over a month now. The butterflies were leaving Wisconsin. The shock phase of Jessie's murder was gradually transitioning to the cold, empty reality of loss. The outpouring of love had run its course. We still had the support of family and our community, yet we felt alone in our profound sadness. Our house was quiet. Our phones were no longer lighting up. People had to get back to their lives and move forward.

After every sign, my heart soared and my hope and faith were rejuvenated for a while. But as time passed between signs, I had to fight to remember, to keep from sinking back into bitter darkness. My mind had trouble retaining what my soul sensed—the incredible truth of Love and Eternity. Rationally, eternal life and the existence of a supreme being were nonsensical and just too good to be true.

But each experience laid another brick in the temple of knowing, and I was getting a little better at it, at living by faith and not by sight.

One of Jessie's best friends, Jackie, was particularly good about staying in touch. She spent much of that first week in July at our house, and she continued to text and visit. She sensed our anguish, and suffered her own. Jessie was older, her big sister, her hero. Jackie missed her badly.

She had come by for another visit—God bless her. And today Jackie was happy and excited.

"You guys, I was in a rush to get to work one day last week. I turned to grab my shoes and noticed a blue butterfly on the toe of one of them. It seemed odd and out of place, in my closet, stuck to my shoe, dead. Having heard your butterfly stories, I thought of Jessie. Then it moved. It was alive. I shook it gently to get it off my shoe but it wouldn't let go. It flapped its wings a little. I opened the door to go outside, thinking it would fly away, but it clung tight. I really had to get going, so I gently picked up the butterfly and cupped it in my hands. It began to flap its wings, but it didn't fly away. Maybe it couldn't fly. Maybe it was sick. I stuffed my feet in my shoes, walked outside, gently placed it on a leaf, and turned to go. When I looked over my shoulder, it was flying away. I realized it could've flown away that whole time. But it didn't, until I released it."

Do butterflies teach us lessons? Do they know of letting go? Do they know love and loss, hope and despair? Or are they just insects?

Is metamorphosis just biology? Or could it be a living metaphor from the other side, to feed hope to those of us trying to make it here?

Are caterpillars aware of their struggle? Are they aware of their ability to transform even as they undergo the transformation? As they crawl free of their broken selves and emerge to leave their exoskeleton behind and fly to the corners of creation...are they conscious of it?

And what about humans? Do we see just how much like caterpillars and butterflies we are?

I don't know. Ask Jackie.

◼ Buck Blodgett
October 15, 2013

In my head every second, but not in my arms. In my heart always, but no longer in our house. Three months ago today, two hours from now, we lost you. You needed help; none came. So sorry. Now you know how deep Mom's love is, from her anguish. Missing you bad, sweetie. See you in our dreams.

OF TATTOOS AND TOMMY

"...The dark that we light,
and the night that we fight..."
—Jessie Blodgett/Ian Nytes, "Love by Proxy"

THE LAST SIGN WAS FADING again. Logic and reason was washing away the deep peace of Spirit as an incoming tide will gradually submerge a rock. I had the memories of the little miracles. But they seemed less real as they drifted further into the past. I still believed I was being shown, from time to time, that Jess was right here with me, but I couldn't hold onto the amazing Peace. I missed her.

No more butterflies. How could there be? It was 39° on the sixth of November in Hartford, Wisconsin, and monarchs migrate to Mexico for the winter.

I was at US Bank depositing more donations into Jessie's memorial fund. I also wanted to visit Donna, the bank manager. She had lost her thirty-eight-year-old son, Tommy, unexpectedly a month earlier.

The teller told me to show Donna my new tattoo. I'm not sure why I'd shown it to the teller in the first place. I was in twelve businesses in Hartford that day, checking donation displays, chatting with employees and owners; I didn't show anyone else my new tattoo of Jessie and a butterfly.

The teller said Donna was considering getting a tattoo of her deceased son, Tommy. So, I wandered over and pulled up my sleeve.

The main feature of my tattoo is a stunning portrait of Jessie. But Donna skipped that and asked, "What's the butterfly for? Is there some story there?"

I told her butterfly story number one.

No sooner did I say the word "butterfly" than Donna cut in with, "That was Jessie." That was the same thing, word for word, our neighbor Peggy said to me at the bottom of our driveway.

Donna then shared her own story.

"My husband and I were visiting Tommy's gravesite last week. A butterfly flew over, circled us both twice, then landed right on Tommy's flowers. Then it rose, circled us again twice, and flew away. A friend later told me butterflies are a common way departed loved ones tell us they're OK."

All week, after hearing from three different people—Joy, Jackie, and Ben—about dreams they had about Jessie in the days following her death, dreams in which all parties independently reported that she seemed stoic rather than her usual happy self, I became worried. Before hearing about their dreams, I thought Jess was happy and free. Now I questioned that. Why were her mom and friends having these dreams?

I didn't used to believe in that stuff. Dreams were just dreams—a restless brain at night. But this ate at me. You have to understand, everything was different now. I didn't know what to believe anymore. I knew there was more than meets the eye in this world now, but what was it really? And was "It" taking care of Jessie and making sure she was happy?

Donna's story came exactly when I needed it. It brought me back from worry to Peace and the Great OKness.

It occurred to me my butterfly stories were not just mine. They were consistently involving others who either had their own experiences or witnessed mine: Peggy at the bottom of our driveway; Charles Benson from TMJ4; Ben on his farm; Chris and Darian and the seashell; my brother Dana at the golf course; Hans with the story of Shannon's driver's test; Ali at the D.A.'s office; Jackie's blue shoe butterfly; and now Donna at the bank.

Were we all seeing and feeling things that weren't there? Were we adding meaning to events that had none? Were we projecting? Interpreting reality in a slanted way because of the trauma we shared?

Were my stories the cause of this? Did they create a chain reaction in which our grief influenced our perception so we could find meaning in the worst tragedy we've known?

I don't know.

But not everyone involved here shared this trauma over Jessie; Charles Benson, Darian, Donna, and Ali never knew her. Were they just reacting to my stories? But Charles, Ben, Ali, and Donna didn't even know of my stories before their butterfly events. And there *were*

82

no stories when Peggy said "that's Jessie." Was something really going on here, glimpses into a hidden Divine pattern?

If so, why did it have to be hidden? And why were we gifted these brief brushes with Creation itself?

Was it all just coincidence?

chapter twenty-one

MOTION TO SEPARATE

"The games that we play…"
—Jessie Blodgett/Ian Nytes, "Love by Proxy"

WE GATHERED AGAIN AT THE Washington County Court-house in West Bend on Tuesday, November 27, at 9:00 a.m. This was the fourth hearing.

At the third hearing back in October, Dan had finally entered his plea—two pleas, actually: not guilty, and not guilty by reason of mental defect.

What was that? I didn't do it, but if I did, I was insane? How does that work?

No admission, no acknowledgement of the reality the Criminal Complaint made so obvious. No sorrow shown for Jess. No giving of answers to the questions that haunted us and stalled our healing. No remorse.

Dan took no responsibility. He offered only his plea, which said to us, "I didn't do it. But if you don't believe me, I did it because I was insane."

District Attorney Mark Bensen later explained: in Wisconsin, a defendant could enter two such pleas. There would be a beginning half of the trial in which the State would have the burden to prove guilt. If the State was successful, the second part of the trial would then be the Defense's burden to prove mental defect.

More frustration. More pain.

He had two chances to get off now. We could win, and then still lose by way of the second plea.

As we rose to leave at the end of that third hearing, something moved me to cross the aisle to Dan's dad, Skip. He saw me coming. I put out my hand, and he put out his. We pulled each other in for a short but emotional hug. No words, just an understanding, a sharing of profound pain and loss, without judgment.

Skip was a mess. His face showed how bad he hurt, not only for his family but for ours. Tears streaked his cheeks and pooled in the worry lines. I didn't know Skip well, only from casual meetings in school hallways during our children's performances. But I saw a picture of him now that made me feel for him, and like him. He wasn't being oppositional or defensive. He wasn't resenting me as a figurehead for the enemy that was coming for his son. He was wide open and vulnerable, and there was honesty in his eyes. It takes a big person to stand there in the face of such circumstances.

This fourth hearing today, was a big day in court, the first real significant event. At that third hearing back in October, the Defense had not only entered a plea, but also a motion Judge Martens would rule on at this fourth hearing—a motion to separate.

The motion to separate asserted the attack on Melissa Richards in the park and the attack on Jessie in our home were two separate crimes that should be tried separately, and the evidence in each should not be considered in the other. Such evidence would be unfairly prejudicial to the defendant. This was the purpose of hearing number four: to decide whether the cases would be tried separately or together.

Judge Martens is a brilliant man. Watching him think on his feet and explain his reasoning was a bit like watching a world-class violinist or an agile athlete—you know immediately you're watching a master. He laid out every consideration, every distinction of the law, every argument of both the State and the Defense, in clear detail. He cited precedent-setting cases from both perspectives.

For the first thirty minutes, everything he said, and the way he said it, seemed to suggest his ruling would fall to the State. If so, the two cases—all their evidence and all their charges—would be tried together. I was nervous but encouraged.

We wanted the two cases joined. The State wanted this for Melissa Richard's case because Dan had admitted he was there in the park, but claimed he was just trying to scare her—implying she's the one who grabbed the knife and started fighting. Jessie's case spoke loudly to Dan's true intent in the park.

In fact, before they connected Dan to Jessie's death, he was only charged with unlawful restraint, possession of a weapon, and aggravated assault in Melissa's case. Attempted murder was added after authorities connected him to Jessie. If Jessie's murder was not allowed as evidence in Melissa's case, the State would have a tough time proving attempted murder.

The State also wanted to use evidence from Melissa Richard's case in Jessie's case. The District Attorney feared Dan would at some point claim "accident" and "consensual sex gone wrong." What other possible defense could he have with all the DNA evidence? He was most definitely there. The attack on Melissa just three days before Jessie's death would render an "accidental" defense in Jessie's case difficult for any jury to believe.

As our hopes rose for a favorable ruling, Judge Martens shifted gears. He spent the second half of the hour presenting arguments from the Defense's point of view.

Our hopes crashed.

He ruled for the motion and separated the two cases.

Looking back, it's easy to see now that Judge Martens did the right thing under the law. He erred on the side of caution, the side of protecting the defendant's rights, and thus ensured there could be no appeal on this sensitive gray point in the event of a conviction.

But in the courtroom that day it didn't feel like the right thing to do.

And so our spirits crashed too. We felt the Judge's ruling would make it even more likely now for the Defense to claim "accident" and drag Jess and her reputation through the mud.

Her voice had been silenced. She could not speak in her own defense. It seemed her killer had all the rights. What rights was she granted, alone in her bed, asleep when the binding began? Where was the protection when all that stood between her precious life and savage death was the hope of mercy from a madman?

More frustration. Anger. Pain.

Judge Martens added a key point at the end, however, and granted us a ray of hope. He said as long as the Defense's assertion remained that "he wasn't there and he didn't do it," the motion to separate would stand. But if they changed their story and suggested "accident" and "consent," then he would reconsider the separation.

Nonetheless, we left the hearing deflated and hurting for the truth, for justice. As we stood to go, Joy and I searched, again, for the defendant's parents, Skip and Laura. We walked toward each other and embraced again, as we did at the third hearing back in October. Skip whispered in my ear, "I'm so sorry for your loss." A bridge was being built, a small light in the blackness.

"IT'S BURNING, IT'S BURNING!"

"So when you're in trouble,
Come to me and I'll be there...
Oh, I swear to you."
—Jessie Blodgett/Ian Nytes, "Letter To Humanity"

BEFORE THE FOURTH HEARING IN November, on a bitter cold and gray Wisconsin day, I had lunch at the Sawmill Inn in Richfield, where the accused used to work. Dr. Karl Lickteig, former chiropractor for the Milwaukee Bucks, had invited me out to lend his support and deliver a $1,215 donation to Jessie's Memorial Fund.

I'd never met Dr. Karl. I didn't tell him when he chose the location that setting foot in the Sawmill, where Jessie's killer used to wash dishes, would send a shiver up my spine. But I welcomed it. I wondered briefly how the food would go down. But going there meant Good would never back down from evil, or let evil affect the way Good lives.

A month earlier, Dr. Karl's wife, Trish, called our clinic. She explained to our receptionist, Chris, that she was planning a surprise anniversary party for her husband—a celebration of his twenty-five years in practice. They heard about Jessie on the news, and several of their patients knew her. Though we had never met, we were chiropractic brethren; they wanted to contribute somehow.

Trish thought instead of paying a band to play at his party, it would be nice to have some of Jessie's musician friends perform, and they would make a contribution to her memorial fund instead. We were touched and readily agreed. Jessie's friends were all in, and we heard the party was a big success.

Dr. Karl emailed me a few weeks later and asked if we could have lunch.

I felt an instant rapport with him. We shared personal stories and beliefs for two hours, like old friends. He told me he knew loss too, and tried to let me know it would be okay.

He told me of his first wife, Paula, the woman who taught him what true love was. She passed seventeen years ago. In her last days, her body succumbing to cancer, morphine drip no longer able to stop the pain, she cried out, "It's burning. It's burning."

Dr. Karl said he held Paula in his arms and prayed with all his heart. He told her he was sending a giant monarch butterfly to lift her up, and the butterfly was going to carry her up and away from the pain. She "sank into peace" almost immediately, he said. To this day, he and his brother and friends see Paula in the butterflies flitting around the golf courses where they play.

Had Dr. Karl heard of my butterfly stories?

There were many meaningful moments in our long conversation over lunch. But it was his butterfly story, not being in the restaurant where Dan used to work, that sent the shiver up my spine. I asked him if he had heard of my own butterfly stories. He had not.

Fifteen degrees outside, our first light snow on the ground, late November in Wisconsin, butterflies long gone for winter now, and still, another butterfly reminder that I wasn't alone on my journey through this life.

◾ Buck Blodgett
December 12, 2013

Just dropped a check at Central Middle School that will establish the permanent Jessie Blodgett Music Scholarship Program. She would be so proud. She would be so happy that she will help get kids started in music. She will live on through their music.

Deeply thankful to everyone who has helped so far.

Other donations have gone and will go to her other passion, fighting male on female violence. Sweetie, I promise we will make you proud and happy with this cause too. You are in our hearts forever, and we will not let you down.

chapter twenty-three

THE BOOK

"Don't listen to 'em, what they say is wrong.
Just walk on by and know that you are strong."
—Jessie Blodgett, "Butterflies"

THREE DAYS AFTER THAT POST, I drove to West Bend to pay another visit to the D.A.'s office. This, however, was not to talk. This time I went to read.

District Attorney Bensen greeted me warmly, as always, and escorted me to the conference room, where a stack of photocopies awaited. It was Dan's book.

The D.A. surprised me a week earlier when he said "yes" to my request to read it. It had been on my mind for months. He smiled, asked if I needed anything else, then reminded me that none of this information should leak out before the trial. He trusted me with key evidence, and left me alone to read.

The book was far from complete. There were bits and pieces, a chapter here, a chapter there. The content was revealing though. The main character in Dan's book was a man named D. He was a schizophrenic with an emerging dark personality. In the book, D beats a victim to death in his bed. Another main character was named Jessica. Jessica appeared to be shaping up to be a future target. Jessica's two parents were pediatricians. The similarities between Dan's book and real life were unsettling.

My stomach tightened as I read, my palms got clammy. In one excerpt, Dan commented on Jessica's parents. He wrote about how foolish and uncaring they were—negligent he seemed to suggest, that they would go away for a weekend and leave a seventeen-year-old girl home alone, free to have D over.

Joy and I sometimes had to attend continuing ed seminars. Jess was a part of every family vacation we ever took; we delighted in showing her the world. The three of us loved being together. But for our work seminars, we sometimes left her home alone for a night.

We trusted her. She was an adult now, and she never violated our trust. The last time she was in trouble was first grade, when the principal called because she had been telling the other kids Santa wasn't real. Nineteen-year-old Jess was increasingly self-sufficient and independent.

I knew most of the general content of the book from the Criminal Complaint. But this one simple sentence about Jessica's parents stuck in my craw. Dan had pushed one of my buttons. How dare this monster, this young and arrogant punk who knew nothing of the world, who fancied himself a rock star because he was in some local production of *Bye Bye Birdie*, how dare he judge my wife and me? How dare he judge me as a father? What did he know about loving a child more than life itself? What did he know about leading her through life, basing every decision you ever made on what would be best for her? How dare this killer, whom I had welcomed into my house, place any of the blame for his heinous crime on my shoulders?

My blood boiled.

The nerve he hit was a big one, because in the gut of this grieving dad, he was right about two simple facts: I wasn't there when Jess needed me, and I did leave her home alone.

For a rare time since her death, I let my mind wander into fantasy. I had a baseball bat. I was in the bushes near his house, waiting for him to come home in the dark. Waiting for Old Testament-style justice. An eye for an eye....

chapter twenty-four

JEWISH FOR "COMFORT"

"Now take a second to breathe,
Be calm 'cause the world is at ease."
—Jessie Blodgett, "Butterflies"

IT WAS FAST BECOMING A throwback Wisconsin winter, a winter from the 1960s and '70s. The bottom dropped out of the temperature in mid-November. The snow flew early and often, and never let up. Old trees creaked when the polar wind blew in from the north. Winter's grip held hard and long, even into the cold, rainy spring.

The days were short now, and the nights long. The pale winter sun dropped below the frozen woodlot across Wayside Drive at 4:30 p.m. We awoke in the dark for work, and drove home from work in the dark, too.

Joy and I sometimes felt like the winter had crept into our hearts. Joy cried every single day, many times a day. I could do nothing but hold her. Nothing I said helped. Nothing lifted her up. I learned to just be silent and hug her until it passed, until next time.

On December 23, 2013, patients Shannon and Jonah brought their eleven-month-old baby boy, Noah, back to the clinic for wellness care. They were a thoughtful young couple, and I suspected they really just wanted to cheer me up before Christmas. I loved little Noah, and they knew it. He was so unique. He never made a sound, barely moved whenever I treated him. He just sat there being. He was so present, the most content, peaceful, little observer you've ever seen.

I adjusted Shannon and Jonah, and then it was Noah's turn. Normally he would let me check and treat him while in his mom's arms, passive and unafraid, just taking it all in. But today, as Shannon held him and came close, he reached out, and for the first time ever, he gave me a hug. He buried his face into my cheek, grabbed around my neck, and wouldn't let go for a full minute.

It was so out of character for Noah. He clung tight to me. Never before had he been demonstrative like this. Then, as I continued to hold him, he suddenly bent sideways and leaned down so fast I almost dropped him. Noah grabbed my blue wristband, the LOVE>hate bracelet I wore in Jessie's memory.

He pulled my arm toward him and pinched the wristband between his thumb and forefinger. He gripped it exactly at the butterfly and pulled it right up to his eye and stared it. Then he released it, turned, and smiled up at me.

The moment was over. Noah leaned into Mom's arms, and went back to being the silent, peaceful observer he always was.

Days later, Shannon told me according to Jewish teaching, Noah means "comfort."

Some say babies are closer to God, their souls haven't forgotten the other side yet. I don't know about that. Maybe Noah does, but he's not talking.

chapter twenty-five

THE NOISE FROM ABOVE

"But that's just me."
—Jessie Blodgett/Ian Nytes, "Letter to Humanity"

THE HOLIDAYS WERE UPON US. The world was getting ready to celebrate, congregate with family, and take time off work to rest and recharge.

We dreaded the coming of Christmas. Joy and I would stay home alone this year. We didn't want to be invited to anyone else's Christmas and have them try to cheer us up. We didn't want to be cheered up. We also didn't want to bring anyone else down and cast a shadow on their holidays. We wanted to have our private space and time to grieve.

There was no tree this year, no ornaments, no presents. And no Jessie.

At 11:05 p.m., I went upstairs to go to bed. Joy and I passed as I left the bathroom and she came in.

When we paused to give each other a kiss, she whispered, "Want to lie down on Jessie's bed with me for a while?"

"That's funny; I was just gonna do that myself." It wasn't too unusual for Joy and me to have the same thought at the same time. She'd been saying what I was thinking for three decades.

As we lay down in Jessie's room it occurred to me we hadn't done this since the days immediately after her death. Where had the time gone?

When Jess died, I had the irrational fear I would forget her, forget the sweet smell of her hair, the sound of her voice and laughter. Lying on her bed with Joy, I could almost see and hear her, as if she were there.

I often lie alone on her bed for that very reason. But it was never long before the visions would come—the binding, the gagging, her struggle, the rape, her terror, her pain. It was the same for Joy. But never would I avoid her room. That would have been like avoiding her. I would lie in her bed and remember the good and the bad, for the rest of my life, if that's what it took for the joy of knowing her to wash away the agony of losing her.

We shared random memories, feelings, and stories, lying there together. I saw again in Joy's eyes the haunting, lonely devastation.

I tried to cheer her up.

"Honey, I saw a post by Tammy, today." Tammy was a good friend to Hans and Laura, and the mom of a murdered daughter, Ashleigh. Two intruders broke into their home in the middle of the night, went to Ashleigh's room, and put a shotgun to her head. The blast woke Tammy. She jumped out of bed and ran toward Ashleigh's room as two masked gunmen passed her in the hallway. The case remains unsolved five years later.

"Tammy posted," I said to Joy, "'*Found another dime in Ash's jeans pocket today…thanks for finding another way to give me a sign, Ash.*' In Tammy's family it's not butterflies; it's dimes. Apparently they find them all the time, in places they shouldn't be. Tammy posted that she's been through Ashleigh's clothes a hundred times, and there was never a dime in those jeans for the past five years."

I was trying to give Joy some hope, make her see that there is an afterlife, my butterfly signs were real, and Jess, or angels, or God, or something was trying to give us comfort. But, already forgetting Noah and succumbing to grief's pull with Christmas looming, I ended this story with, "It's been a while since I've had a sign. Wish I could get one.…"

Joy then slipped into a memory about the dreams everyone had about Jessie after her death. Joy had them too. She saw how sullen Jessie was in her dreams, and thought she was hanging around because she was worried about us. Joy said, "We're okay, honey. Just go to the Light." Joy's dreams stopped that night. We learned later that Jackie and Ben's also stopped about that time, too.

Within a second of Joy's story ending, a sound came from above, right out of the light fixture on the ceiling. It was loud, distinct, and unmistakable. Descriptive words fail, but it sounded half electrical and half like a voice—a long loud tone, almost like a person saying "UUUNNNHHH" for a full five seconds. The light never blinked on and off. It worked just fine.

Joy has always had some fear about ghosts and the dark side, fears I don't struggle with. I knew this would rattle her, so I turned to comfort her.

"Honey, think about it. We lie here for the first time in half a year. I just said I wanted another sign. You remembered telling Jess to go to the Light. We then hear a sound coming from the light, a sound we've never heard in fifteen years here. If that was from the dark side, it would've happened when you were alone, not when we were together."

Joy was still unnerved, so we left Jessie's room and curled up tight in our own bed. She finally drifted off to sleep, but I was wide awake, touched by another glimpse of the beyond. This was a whole new level of sign.

I lay there in fascination for hours, mind wandering all over, to things like Morgan Freeman's *Through the Wormhole* TV series. One episode in particular explored breakthrough thinking in modern physics. A minority of world class physicists now theorize that there are eleven dimensions. Well, we can sense four, the three involving space (X, Y, and Z axes), plus time. Some of us, perhaps, have varying abilities involving a sixth sense (intuition, déjà vu, prophecy, etc.).

But what are those other six dimensions? Where are they? Could there be energetic phenomena all around us that we are mostly unable to sense with our vision, hearing, taste, smell, or touch, as the *Wormhole...* suggested?

I remembered hearing in chiropractic school twenty-two years ago there was enough latent energy in a cubic yard of empty space to power New York City for a day.

Why should humans believe we can sense all that exists? We can't see in the dark like bats, smell someone's trail days later like a bloodhound, feel something move underwater from a hundred feet away, like a fish, or sense a drop of blood in the ocean from a quarter mile, like a shark. These creatures all sense reality differently than us, because we all have different sensory organs. Who says we humans sense reality the way it is?

Then there was the episode, *String Theory,* in which physicists postulated that everything is literally connected by tiny invisible strings, or bands of energy.

Finally, in another episode, *Living Space,* physicists theorized the universe is alive and intelligent. It has every characteristic biologists use to define life. It has the ability to reproduce, that is, make new stars and planets. It has a birth (the Big Bang), a lifespan, and a death, and even a circulatory system and a central nervous system. And it has incalculable functional capacity infinitely beyond that of a quantum supercomputer.

Quantum supercomputers get really interesting. Instead of arranging lots of zeroes and ones in staggering amounts of combinations to compute and store ridiculous amounts of data (like our current binary computers do), quantum computers use subatomic particles to compute and store information. Scientists are learning how to "massage" subatomic particles just right in order to get them to carry out the calculations they want the particles to perform.

When we perfect this science, quantum computers will have incalculably more computing power than our current binary computers. In the *Wormhole's* episode, *Living Space,* it suggested the living universe has infinitely more computing power than these emerging quantum computers.

I'm not sure about all that, as fascinating as I find it. I just felt like God knew Christmas was coming, knew about my deep sadness and despair. Was I given two signs, two encounters with the Divine, on the same day for that very reason?

I had the crazy feeling the biggest quantum supercomputer in all of history was Love, and It knew me and loved me too.

Dear Jess,

Tonight I'll watch the Year in Review shows you and I watched the past three years. I'll miss talking with you about what happened in the world this year, and where the world's going. I'll miss talking about what happened in our lives, and where we're going. We used to set goals for the new year, and look back at how we did with last year's goals. I remember when I last looked in my underwear drawer at my 2013 goals in early July. Most of them were already accomplished. Half of them involved you. I remember thinking, what a banner year for our family. Your bright future was really taking shape. A lifetime of hard work and planning by Mom and me was starting to pay off. The three of us were excited and happy.

Then you were gone.

I have no goals for 2014, except to honor you, love you, and stay true to your legacy. To have your death have an even bigger positive impact on the world than your life did, God willing.

I love you forever, sweetie.

LOVE> hate.

And Love will do some serious ass kicking on hate in the years to come.

chapter twenty-six

THE ICE CREAM TRUCK

"Now it's five o'clock,
I've been up all night."

—Jessie Blodgett, "Music"

WE SURVIVED CHRISTMAS. BUT NOW it was New Year's Eve, which I was dreading more than every holiday, except Jessie's birthday.

I watched the *Year in Review* shows alone. Every hour, a different country in a different time zone would ring in the New Year on *CNN*. People around the world were making resolutions, partying like there was no tomorrow, dreaming their dreams for the future. None of them knew Jessie. The world didn't even know it lost her, didn't care. I nodded off in our living room recliner as the ball dropped in NYC.

At 11:05 p.m., I was jolted awake by a "bam!"

Did I really hear that? It sounded as if I had taken my fist and smacked the wooden dining room table. I jumped up to check on Joy.

"Honey, did you hear that?" she said. I could hear the quiver in her voice, even though she was upstairs.

"Yeah, was that you?" I asked on my way up.

"No. It sounded like a big crash on the roof right above me. I was dozing off. It startled me."

"Honey, we've been waiting fifteen years for one of those big limbs to fall on the roof. I'm sure that's what it was."

Our yard is full of hundred-year-old oaks and maples. It was the yard and the trees that drew us to the house in the first place. But we trimmed all the big limbs away from the house. It would have taken a seventy-mph-wind to break one and blow it onto the roof over our bedroom.

"Don't worry. I'll go out in the morning and check the yard and the roof."

We hopped into bed and drifted off.

At about 5:00 a.m., I woke with a start from another "bam!" I looked over; Joy was up, looking around. She'd been up all night. This was the seventh "bam!" she told me. I had slept right through the others (thanks to the earplugs I use). The first one came from the roof above our bed. One sounded like it came from the roof above Jessie's bedroom. Another sounded like it came from the basement, one from the stairway, another from an exterior wall. They had come from all over the house. I couldn't believe what she was telling me.

The strangest part was she didn't seem scared. I lay there in the dark for a long time, staring at the ceiling, hoping she'd drift off again. It was my turn to be unnerved. I rolled over and looked at the alarm clock: 5:40 a.m. I was getting up in an hour.

All was quiet and still, and I was nearly asleep again. And then I heard it. Music. Bells maybe, almost like the ice cream truck in summer, but not quite an organized song, just tinkling. I didn't want to move. I wasn't sure if Joy was sleeping, and I didn't want to wake her. So I listened for a bit, and then whispered, "Do you hear that too?"

"Yes," she replied.

Anticipating her fear, for there was no reasonable, rational explanation for the music, I started to calm her.

But she stopped me and said, "It's okay. It's fine. I asked God for a sign last night," and she rolled over.

Well, it was not fine with me! I got up to search the house. The music stopped as soon as my feet hit the floor. I hurried downstairs and searched everywhere, checked all the doors and windows, and found nothing out of order. Then I heard her call down.

"It's okay, honey. It was the chimes."

"What chimes?" I called back. I was angry now, maybe because I was scared and that's what men do when they're scared; they get mad and ready to fight. Or maybe I was angry because I had lost control of my world, or because I couldn't understand or explain this craziness, or because Joy was suddenly okay with it all.

"The chimes in the mudroom," she added.

I didn't know we had chimes in the mudroom. And I didn't know how they could be going off if we did.

I went to the mudroom. Hanging by the sliding glass door in plain view were the chimes. I recognized them now; my brother Dana had given them to us to remember Jessie. They had hung there silently for months. The steel gray chimes had a big, beautiful four-inch monarch butterfly perched on top. There was no wind to move them, of course. They were inside.

I checked the vent below. Warm air was pouring out, same as it always does, but the chimes were perfectly still—not enough airflow to budge them. I rattled them with my finger, not yet convinced Joy was right. It was the same tinkling musical sound I had heard minutes before in bed. I checked all the doors and windows to see if there was any way a breeze could blow in. Nothing.

I went back upstairs to ask Joy about this sign she asked for—a little freaked out and ticked off that suddenly she was the one accepting that signs are real and good. To my amazement, she was sleeping peacefully.

The butterfly chimes have hung in the mudroom for eighteen months now. That morning was the only time we've ever heard them, ringing us into the new year.

chapter twenty-seven

FIND ANOTHER WAY

"Butterflies under my skin,
Butterflies trying to do me in.
It's making me crazy,
It's been happening lately."
—Jessie Blodgett, "Butterflies"

I WENT OUTSIDE THE NEXT morning. There were no broken tree limbs anywhere. Part of me, the part deep inside where you just know things, knew I'd find nothing. But I had to check anyway because of that other part of me, the reasonable, rational, common sense part that doesn't believe in miracles. When Joy woke up, I made her go down to the mudroom and rattle the chimes while I lay on our bed.

Yep, same sound.

It occurred to me in the sober light of day that perhaps our house was contracting during the frigid night. Do houses do that? It was one of the coldest nights that winter. That wouldn't fully explain for me, though, the seven loud "bams" when we had never had one in fifteen years. (There have been other frigid days since we moved in.) And on the same night Joy asked God for a sign? And it certainly didn't explain the butterfly chimes going off indoors.

Joy and I did New Year's Day like we did Christmas: home alone. We had gone back to work a week after our daughter was taken from us and had not missed a day since, except half days for court hearings. As difficult as it was, the alone time was important—to let down and allow ourselves to grieve.

I spent much of the day watching the college bowl games. She spent it playing computer games. We basically vegged out, recharged, and embraced the sadness.

Around midafternoon she came to me. "Honey, I don't want to leave, but I don't know if I can stay in this house anymore."

That was all. No conversation. No big explanation. I could see in her eyes she needed me to understand. She was trapped in an impossible choice: to stay in a house where scary things might happen at any time, or to leave the home that held all the memories of her lost daughter.

I believed if Jess was still with us in spirit she would be with us anywhere we went. Still, I felt a connection to her here and wanted to stay.

This is where she grew up. This is where I scratched her back and told her nutty stories while she giggled and drifted off to sleep. This is where she went through hell alone, and left her body behind.

But I knew if Joy couldn't stay here, well, I'd have to support her. I gave it an hour, and snuck upstairs to have a little talk with Spirit.

"God, Jesus, Jess, angels, Whoever.... Thank you! Thank you for the amazing signs. They've changed everything for me. I get it. You're real, you're here, and you won't share the whole mystery with me, but you're giving me hope. I will never doubt again. Please keep them coming. They're all I have to carry me.

"But…can you leave Joy out of it? Keep them between you and me. I want to stay here, and you're freaking her out.

"Can you please find another way?"

We've not heard another sound in the house since. All quiet on Wayside Drive.

◪ Buck Blodgett
January 15, 2014

Six months ago today, Jess.

Holly's poem says it best:

"Half my heart died with you, the other half aches constantly for you."

But…that other half is ten times stronger than it ever was, because of you. That other half is ten times kinder than it ever was, because of you.

Because of you, my brave young woman of the earth, as Ian called you, I love more, I care more, I appreciate more, I reach out more, I see more clearly, and I live more fully. Because of you, Butterfly, I BELIEVE in the Butterfly Effect—that every single thing I do MATTERS! And not just for me, but for EVERYONE. And not just for now but for FOREVER.

You touched many, sweetie, and you continue to. Because of you, The LOVE>hate Project was born. Your body is gone, "disappeared by hands of destruction" as Ben said, but they could not destroy your spirit, your heart, your goodness, your beauty, and your love.

I miss touching you, sweetie, but I know you're here. You've made that clear as only you could. Because of you I live one hundred percent present and on purpose in this world, but I long to join you in the other and see you again.

chapter twenty-eight

A MESSAGE FROM JESSIE

"I'll be here...I'll be here for you."
—Jessie Blodgett/Ian Nytes, "Letter to Humanity"

IN JANUARY OF 2014, MILWAUKEE was in the midst of the second coldest winter on record, and I was on the razor's edge. Broken but inspired. Up and down. Every emotion, good and bad, boiling inside.

January 19 dawned cold, but unexpectedly clear. Patches of soft pink and orange pastels streaked the winter sky as the sun rose over Pike Lake.

I crunched around the frozen forest trails alone, breath crystallizing in the frigid air. I recalled two months earlier, when eighty people gathered here to walk and remember, and I was struck, once again, by how Jessie's story was touching so many.

My awareness of the still small voice was growing. I heard it best on these hikes alone in the woods. In nature, inspired thoughts flowed freely.

A month had passed—again—since my last sign. As always, the amazing magical presence of the Great Artist, the Master of time, space, and events, was again receding into memory.

On January 30, I got a private message from Laura Gruber. When I entered the Facebook world last August, over one hundred of Jessie's friends "friended" me. Laura was one of them. I didn't really know her, but she knew me. Everyone in Hartford knew Joy and me now.

Laura's message was: *I have something important to share with you. It's too personal and too long for Facebook. Do you have an email address?*

My curiosity was piqued.

The next morning, I arrived at my office at 8:30 a.m., a half hour ahead of patients. I powered on my laptop, anxious to check my email. Laura had sent me a letter.

Dear Buck,

I'm not sure where to begin with this, but after speaking with Ian yesterday, he encouraged me to contact you.

I'm not sure why, but God has blessed me with a special talent. I receive dreams, visions and messages from God, angels, and guides. Guides are people we love who have crossed over. In my writing I've received a message from your beautiful daughter, Jessie. I was asked to share with you and Ian. I was reluctant. Not knowing you very well, I didn't want you to think I was crazy. The message is short but insightful and profound.

This is Jessie's dictation to me on January 22, 2014.

LOVE>hate…. Thank you, Laura, for everything—for the ornament, prayers, and for being there for my parents. Hugs to Ian, but he might not believe you. Song, up all night (love and laughter). Such a good friend. Dan IS sick. Pray for his mental health. My parents will understand someday the messages in my home.

Ian said he had a dream and Jess was in it—just staring at him—and it kinda freaked him out. I explained our loved ones will pull away if they think their presence is not being received in a positive way, and then look for another vessel to send a message. In this case: me. I work with Ian part-time at Walmart, and Jess knows my daughter, Emily, and I have contact with you. When I asked him about the "up all night" reference, he said he has been staying up all night working on the LOVE>hate web page.

The message to Ian was Jessie's way of saying: I am with you; I see what you're doing.

Jessie also told me she is free and without pain. She, of all people, would know Dan's mental state. In Heaven they have no hostility or grudges. I believe she wants you to pray for him to help you through your journey. To really focus on love not hate as a way for you to find your own inner peace so you can move forward. The more you focus on LOVE you will find you are embraced by positive energy, and you will please Jessie. Live your life to its fullest—have inner peace and keep her memory alive with everything you do (CD, scholarships, and so on); that's what she wants.

The last thing she said: **My parents will understand someday; messages in my home.**

I interpret that as one of two things. Either there are other clues that might have been overlooked pertaining to the case, or she is with you in your home and sending messages and signs of her presence.

I love your daughter.

She came to me again five days later. This is the dictation I took from her on January 27, 2014. She was very determined to get this to you.

Hello, keep writing, letter sounds good. SEND IT RIGHT AWAY! Please :D Tell them I love them so much. I am there. Look for signs, noises, and maybe shadows. Cuddle with me, Dad. I always loved our time together. You are so strong please be there for Mom. I am okay/no pain, happy camper :D. Butterflies everywhere. I will share them with you. Don't second-guess yourself when you see, hear, or feel my presence. It is me. Believe. I love you.

This one's easy to interpret. She is with you, and okay. You must be using a blanket or going to a special spot of hers. She is with you at those times. Happy camper must mean either just that phrase, or it's an outdoors reference, loving nature and feeling free. The last line is self-explanatory!

I hope you find peace in this. I always pray that God will only guide me to positive things and if it were not for Ian, I would have sat on these messages in fear of what you might think.

If you have any questions or concerns I am here; otherwise, I will give you your space.

Laura Gruber

It took me twenty minutes to read this letter. I had to keep stopping to absorb it. Patients would begin arriving soon. I didn't care. The tears started before I finished the third sentence—where Laura said she receives messages. I knew instantly what was coming, and the deep feeling of profound peace, the overwhelming Great OK-ness, once again, swept through my body.

How could Laura Gruber know anything about the messages in my home?

How could she have correctly interpreted the "happy camper" reference to "loving nature and feeling free?" No one except me, not even Joy, knew that every single time Jess and I had gone foraging together last summer she had danced around and exclaimed how free she felt in nature.

And how could she possibly know this: The day before I opened this email was the worst day of my life—even worse than the actual day we lost Jess.

I had hit rock bottom.

The shock phase was over, and all that was left was emptiness.

The day before I opened Laura Gruber's email, I went up to Jessie's room. I stood by the side of her bed. I imagined her lying there, sleeping peacefully…. And then, I bent over, put my arm around her, and gave her a kiss on the head, as if she were actually there.

Even though I was alone, it was kind of awkward. But something about it felt really good, too, and I ended up hugging "her" for a full five minutes. Then, I grabbed the flannel shirt hanging on her bedpost, the shirt that still smelled like her, the one she wore so much in her last days. I climbed onto her bed with the shirt and, using it like a blanket, I snuggled with "her" for a half hour. I talked to her, told her how I felt, and let memories of her soothe my pain. And I imagined she talked back, speaking words of comfort and wisdom.

How could Laura Gruber have known that?

I didn't even tell Joy I spent a half hour snuggling with our murdered daughter on the worst day of my life.

Cuddle with me, Daddy. I always loved our time together.

That dictation from Jess to Laura was written on January 27, just as I was beginning my descent.

Funny thing—Divine timing.

f Buck Blodgett

January 30, 2014

We cannot hate the murderers, the rapists, the thieves, the abusers, the selfish, the greedy. They are sick.

If we want to heal the world, we must start with the sick. If we hate them, we add to the aggregate hate in the world, we join their side. We MUST find it in ourselves to love them, to pray for them, and mean it. This is VERY important! LOVE>hate. We must find it in us to increase our Love, to add to the aggregate Love in the world.

Don't get me wrong. I'm NOT saying, "Let them out of jail, feel sorry for them, be lenient on them, don't punish them, or don't put them away and protect the public." I'm not saying that. I'm saying LOVE THEM.

No, I'm not crazy.

THREE QUESTIONS

"It's no surprise that I've got…butterflies."
—Jessie Blodgett, "Butterflies"

I SLAPPED SOME WATER ON my face and began treating patients. I was elated, euphoric. This latest message was the greatest sign yet. I felt like I had been given a new level of blessing.

Every patient encounter and every staff interaction was magical that day. I loved people again. I loved life again. This wasn't a butterfly, this wasn't a "bam," this wasn't unexplained music in the night. This was a message from Jessie herself, and it contained things only she would know.

How can one lose the most precious thing in life to a brutal act of violence and feel like I was feeling? In a natural world of reasoning and physical reality one cannot, unless one is crazy. But in a mysterious world where the supernatural becomes real, it is simple. The astoundingly good news that we are not done when we die, that our loved ones may be physically gone, but are happy, free, and with us in spirit forever…. Well, that changes everything.

It was the dead of winter in the northern Great Lakes region. The butterflies were long gone, a thousand miles away in Mexico. But Jess said to me in her dictation to Laura Gruber: **"Butterflies everywhere. I will share them with you. Believe."**

I promised her I would.

I grabbed my iPad and left my office. It was time to treat patients.

The butterfly gifts from patients had stopped coming in a couple months ago, but the first three people I treated that morning brought me the following items: a colorful ceramic butterfly on a flower, a colored pencil sketch of a brilliant monarch framed in glass, and a 2014 Calendar with, you guessed it, huge beautiful butterflies on every page.

I emailed Laura Gruber on my first break: *Can we have coffee?*

She replied within the hour. We arranged to meet after work.

Later that day, Laura walked into the back of McDonald's. I was waiting with my cup of coffee. She was petite, with long, black hair and a presence too big for her physical frame.

She stuck out her hand. "Hi, I want you to know I don't do this for money," she said nervously before she even sat down.

I liked her immediately.

She got right to the point. "I seem to have this gift. I don't want it. For fourteen years, departed people have talked to me and asked me to give messages to their loved ones. I journal as they dictate. They bother me, and it builds, often in the middle of the night, until I get up, grab a pen, and write down what they say."

I couldn't believe what I was hearing. Again.

"Five years ago, after my mother passed, I said, 'Enough. I'm not doing it anymore.' I put my pen and journal down one day, and didn't pick it up again until last week, when your daughter came to me. She was so persistent and determined I couldn't ignore her. She was extremely strong, so strong she came to the front of the line ahead of my own mother. But she was very polite, respectful, and kind. I love your daughter."

Laura told me how she first discovered her gift, how it scared her. She told me she doubted herself and feared she would make a mistake and hurt someone. She told me she learned others have this gift, too, and she began to read books and learn how to interpret her encounters.

As I spoke to her accuracy, her confidence grew, and I saw before me a person who had found her life's calling and had finally emerged from the closet to claim her gift.

That was the first of many meetings with Laura, the first of many messages, and, though neither of us knew it at the time, it was also the beginning of a valuable alliance for The *fledgling* LOVE>hate Project.

I left McDonald's. My mind raced a hundred miles per hour as I reviewed the events of the day, starting with the email and ending with meeting Laura Gruber. What an incredible day January 31 turned out to be. I was high on the stunning possibility that Jess had communicated with me, but it was just too beyond belief. So, on that

119

two-minute drive home, I formed three questions for Jessie. Test questions.

"Honey, and God, if this is real please confirm it for me. I'm sorry for doubting again. You have gone so far beyond what I originally asked for that terrible night in the hotel when I said—*I'm gonna need more than one sign this time*—but I know you understand. You have to understand, God; *you made me this way*. If this is really true, answer these questions:

1. How many minutes did it take for you to die, sweetie?
2. What should I do about R?
3. What does God want me to do next?

Question number one was the foremost thing on my mind since her death. How much did she suffer? How long did it take? Joy and I even Googled strangulation and learned the victim usually loses consciousness in about fifteen seconds. Then another minute or so of sustained pressure is required to kill them.

Question three might seem obvious, but when you go from an atheist to a believer in one night, and that happens because your daughter was murdered, you want to know what you're supposed to do next.

Question two makes no sense to you yet, but I will get to that....

If I received answers to these questions it would be beyond coincidence, and all doubt would be gone.

In bed that night, I repeated my three questions. I half hoped they would be answered in my dreams. Drifting off, my mind flashed back to New Year's Day, when Joy said she might not be able to stay in the house. I had asked God, Jess, or the angels to please keep the signs coming, but leave Joy out of it. Find another way. I guess you could say they did that.

chapter thirty

ROCK BOTTOM

"Keep your chin up, 'cuz you can't give up yet."
—Jessie Blodgett, "Butterflies"

I CONTEMPLATED THE THREE QUESTIONS on my drive to work the next morning.

I wanted to memorize them and watch to see if they would be answered. If I could really communicate with Jess, or God, or angels, then they would answer me.

Tears soaked my eyelids, as they so often did when I drove to work, alone, listening to her CD. Lost in a memory, it suddenly occurred to me what I really cared most about was not the answers to those three questions, but this fourth one: *Honey, will we see each other again when I die?* I had the strange feeling this question was given to me. It felt more important than my test questions.

Three days passed.

The euphoria of the message from Jess was already slipping away, as usual. And the darkness that descended on me four days earlier returned.

I had always been pretty steady, pretty solid my whole life; generally happy, and eternally optimistic. I prided myself on being in control of my attitude and having a mentally disciplined, positive outlook on life. Now, I felt like a different person. I felt bipolar, the opposite of the pre-murder me. I was riding the highest of highs, then sinking to the lowest of lows.

How could I lose this life-changing awakening and new knowledge so fast? Just three days ago, I knew I would never doubt again. But now, for the first time in my life, I was gripped by a depression so strong I felt powerless against it. I thought I had grieved fully, with open eyes and an open heart. I thought I had done well for seven months. Why now?

◼ Buck Blodgett

February 3, 2014

Bottomless pain....
Deep despair....
Busted heart....
Strength gone....
Rock bottom.
Sorry everyone. Don't wanna "attention grab," but if I don't share darkness, too, I'm a liar.

The comments poured in. My friends buried me in compliments and encouragement. They don't all know it, but their collective response got me through; I love them all for that. I love my wife too.

122

Her response was the first one at the top of the long comment chain. She posted: *I'm calling you right now….*

Another week passed. The blackness continued, but I knew I was loved by many, including Jess and God, and someway, somehow I would be given what I needed to make it through this and come out stronger, more humble, and wiser. I was metal being forged in fire and hammered into something more useful and beautiful.

A friend said, "I love you. Hold onto that."

And I did. I held onto hope.

But with each passing day, the three questions remained unanswered.

On February 12, I checked my email and found a message from Monica, my sister-in-law in Alberta. Monica had never emailed me before. We only saw each other every few years.

Good Morning Buck,

I hope you don't mind me mentioning Jessie in this way. I don't want to upset you, but…. I booked a reading with this medium, Lee. Losing both my mom and brother last year was hard, and I was hoping to connect with them. Lee asked me not to give her any information…so she knew nothing about my family or me.

Most of my session was spent with my deceased brother, Bruce. Lee brought up specific illnesses and injuries Bruce had, so I am pretty sure it was him. Okay…now…at the end of our session Lee said my brother was motioning that there was someone younger there whose name started with a J…. Lee said J wasn't settled in the spirit world because she still had unfinished business here on earth. The medium said she could feel the shock of this person's passing in her whole body because it really wasn't J's time to go. Lee said this was odd; she has talked to thousands of people/spirits, and she had never felt so much shock.

Lee said she sensed all the goodness about Jessie, the way she loved people, the way she was so confident and outgoing, how she would have gone on to make the world a better place. She said Jessie was still being held here; Jessie still has work left to do here before she can become settled on the other side.

And then this next part blew me away. I actually wrote it down. Lee said your work with an organization that addresses violence against women will help you heal, and give meaning to Jessie's life and death.

Now I was getting messages through a stranger, a medium, fifteen hundred miles away in a different country mentioning our organization, which hadn't even gone public yet. Skeptical Me thought she must have done one heck of an Internet search. But Newly Awakened Me was intrigued.

I hit reply.

Hi Monica,

First question: How did it go from "J" to Jessie? Was she fishing for letters? Asking for names? Or did she just out of the blue name a "J" and you knew it was Jess? Second question: Did you really tell her absolutely nothing about your family before she said all this about "J"?

Monica replied on February 13, 2014.

Okay. Answers. I told her nothing about my family. I wasn't even thinking about Jessie that day. Lee wasn't fishing for names, but she does use letters, then said there was someone younger with Bruce and asked if I knew anyone who passed recently whose name started with a "J."

I did just remember one thing...the medium brought up the number 2. She held up two fingers and asked if that number was significant. I didn't know what that meant. Nicole said we had seen her two Christmases ago. I don't know....

Oh my God.... I replied immediately upon reading Monica's email: *Please try to remember, very important: Did she bring up the number "2" at the time Jess was coming through, or not?*

Monica's reply minutes later: *The number 2 came from Jessie.*

There it was. The answer to my first question: *How many minutes did it take you to die, sweetie?*

This was unexpected. I meant to test Laura Gruber, and this whole "messages from beyond" thing. But I never expected an answer from someone else. It was too much for my rational mind to believe. Maybe I was adding meaning where there was none again. But my spirits rose once more.

"YES"

*"I will allow no man to narrow and degrade my soul by
making me hate him."*
—Booker T. Washington (on the Men's
Room door at the Perc Place.)

BLACK FEBRUARY, ROLLER-COASTER FEBRUARY, rolled on. I knew I had to grant "being" to the emotions and embrace them, and choose to function productively despite them. *What you resist persists.* But, man, the darkness was bad.

Laura Gruber emailed me again. We decided to meet for coffee, this time at our local coffee shop, the Perc Place. It was becoming my second home; my new meeting grounds for The LOVE>hate Project; the hatching place for hopes, dreams, and plans to change the world.

While I waited for Laura, I slipped into the men's room. Standing at the urinal, I read the wall: *Accept that some days you are the pigeon and some days you are the statue.* I bent over the sink to wash my hands and saw: *Changing the toilet paper does NOT cause brain damage.* And then reaching for paper towel: *Never put YOUR key to happiness in someone else's POCKET.*

There's a lot of humor and wisdom in the men's room at the Perc Place. I try to use it. I try to accept what happens. I change the roll when I use the last piece. And I don't give my key to happiness to anyone else.

…But sometimes people just take your key when it wasn't given. Like Dan did.

Jess loved all the sayings on the walls. Maybe that's why she painted quirky, thought-provoking, inspirational sayings all over her bedroom, and pinned buttons on her fair trade purse from Ecuador:

I'm in this world to change this world.
War is not healthy for children and other living things.
SLUTWALK MILWAUKEE: rape is the only crime where the victim becomes the accused.

I imagine Dan read all the sayings on Jessie's purse and walls, too.

Laura arrived and we sat down to coffee.

"You must be asking questions," Laura said. Jessie had visited her again, this time in a dream. "Well, the answer is 'yes.' Do you know what that means? I hate messages like this, when I don't know what they mean."

I was surprised and excited again by Laura's statement that I must be asking questions. But I had no idea what "yes" meant. *How many minutes did it take you to die? What should I do about R? What does*

God want me to do next? None of my questions could be answered with a "yes."

I left disappointed.

The doubts crept in as I drove home. My three test questions tumbled around in my head. Maybe Laura had made some good guesses in our first meeting, gotten lucky, and my imagination had done the rest. Was Monica's "2" my imagination filling in the blanks as well?

I turned slowly onto Wayside Drive. And then it struck me.

I pulled into our driveway, stopped, and texted Laura as fast as I could: *I forgot about the fourth question: Will I ever see you again, Jess?*

There it was, the deep and indescribable feeling of peace and Love beyond all understanding, the Great OKness.

chapter thirty-two

CEDAR SPRINGS

"You gotta take a risk for every day
And throw the rest away."
—Jessie Blodgett, "Overnight"

SCOTT, FROM JESSIE'S NATURE GROUP of friends, was one of the first kids to walk up our driveway the night of her murder. He was an introspective young man. It was Scott, Caleb, and Jessica who took Jess winter camping for the first time.

Winter camping was a huge win in her life. She was very proud of surviving that frigid weekend alone at Devil's Lake State Park. The bottom had dropped out of the thermometer that weekend, and those kids, all alone in the normally popular park, stuck it out, kept each other warm, kept each other positive, and braved the worst days of that winter in a tent.

Jess did not tolerate physical discomfort, much less pain, very well. That weekend with Scott, Caleb, and Jessica was a milestone for her.

Scott and the nature group brought a framed photo to Joy and me after she passed. It was from the weekend at Devil's Lake State Park. All the kids were bundled up, pink-faced, and smiling ear-to-ear. I treasure that photo.

Scott had texted me in the morning: *Wanna come to church with me Sunday?*

I'm not sure why he asked. I had only connected with him a couple times since Jess died. I don't recall having discussed spirituality or religion with him.

I texted back: *Yes.*

I hadn't been to church since the mid-eighties in New Jersey, and not much at all throughout my life. I had always been open and spiritual in my own way, but not religious at all.

But things had completely changed for me. I had been humbled by life and death, broken by loss, and pulled time and again from the wreckage by the Great OKness. I was ready.

My phone rang. It was Scott, responding to my text.

"Yes?" he said with surprise.

"Yes, Scott, yes. I'd like to go to church with you." I chuckled at his surprise.

We arrived at Cedar Springs at about 9:20 a.m. on Sunday, February 23. Service started in ten minutes. "Our God Is an Awesome God" was playing as we shuffled in, my all-time favorite spiritual song. I hadn't heard that song since I was last in church in New Jersey. I got a little déjà vu and chuckled quietly, thinking, *now He's just messing with me.*

Like a typical teenager (well, he was twenty-one), Scott abandoned his guest (me) when he spotted a friend. I saw coffee and went for it. As the brew plinked into the bottom of my Styrofoam cup, a voice boomed out from behind.

"Hey, you can't have coffee till your third service here!"

It was Pastor John Bass, a big bear of an East Coaster whose intimidating size was belied by the kindness and wisdom in his face.

I shot back, "Then I'll only fill it one-third full. Will that work?"

He laughed.

I was immediately off my defense. John had that effect on people. He wanted nothing from me; just the chance to laugh and serve. John took me as I was, just like God does.

I felt strangely at home that day at Cedar Springs. I cried a lot. Every song and word seemed to be for Jessie and me. And near the end of the service I felt her presence over my right shoulder, warming my ear and cheek, and my heart. It was her. She was there. I know it.

Don't believe me; call it my imagination. I don't care. I know it makes no sense. I wouldn't have believed me either, until now. I've felt her many times since, but I feel her best at Cedar Springs. Not sure why.

On the drive home, Scott said, "Buck, I'd really like you to meet my pastor. John is a really great guy. I just feel like you two should connect."

"I just met him."

"No, I mean you should get together sometime. Maybe have a cup of coffee or something."

I didn't say it out loud, but in my head I thought, *Scott, I just went to church for the first time in thirty years! I don't want to have coffee with your pastor.*

"Really, you guys should get together."

The new me was more social than ever, saying yes to life, making new friends, renewing old ones, living one hundred percent like Jessie did. Every second mattered. Every person mattered. She would have been proud. I just wish I had lived like this when she was still with me.

So when Pastor John called a few days later, I said, "Yes."

We became fast friends. He became The LOVE>hate Project's biggest fan and promoter. The first time we met, I showed him our three-minute video (slides of Jess, her songs playing in the background, and graphic images of male on female violence). The video would become the official trailer for our project and play at the beginning of every LOVE>hate presentation—telling the story of her life, death, and legacy.

John was moved by the video. "You better get ready," he said.

"For what?"

"To travel. To speak. You're going to be showing this video all over the country, telling Jessie's story, and teaching people your amazing story of Love and forgiveness.

If it wasn't for Jess going winter camping, I wouldn't have gone to church with Scott. If it wasn't for Scott, I wouldn't have met Pastor John. And if it wasn't for John, my understanding of what was going on here would not have expanded beyond my own myopic view.

Another resource had found me, found The Project. Pastor John, in the months to come, would interview me in front of his whole church, liken his "discovery" of me to reporters discovering Mother Teresa, and talk about The LOVE>hate Project like it was sent straight from Jesus. He'd have me lead all the men in the congregation in taking the Real Man Pledge, and rally his many troops to support our breakout events when we could finally go public.

But the ups and downs continued....

▪ Buck Blodgett
March 15, 2014

Eight months ago today, sweetie.... Missing you, thinking of you, feeling you in my heart. Going through the stages, waiting on the Light to come back, trusting.

Thanks for finding ways. I know now we'll meet again, but from here it seems impossible sometimes. I know now you're here, but from here it doesn't usually seem like it.

Mom and I will never stop loving you. Just wish you could come home from college with your friends, play your piano, make a mess, rustle my hair....

chapter thirty-three

JESUS CALLING

"When the student is ready, the Master appears."

—Zen saying

IN LATE FEBRUARY, I WAS working on my laptop at our dining room table. My favorite red and black coffee mug sat within easy reach. Tink, our seventeen-year-old tabby was curled up in my lap. I was still wrestling with rock bottom, and preparing to pay the monthly bills for our LLC when my phone lit up with a text from an old friend, Barbie Orban.

Barbie lived across the street from me in my childhood neighborhood. She was the tenth kid in a ten-kid family. Her dad left when she was three. Her mom worked nights. The five oldest kids were grown up and gone, and the five youngest were left alone to fend for themselves.

The police were at Barbie's house many nights. As a party house, it was off the charts. It was no place for a little girl.

Barbie told me after we reconnected that people still comment nostalgically about what a great party house she grew up in. They have no idea what it was like for young Barbie. She was abused, assaulted, neglected. A dropout in seventh grade, and then a runaway, Barbie was among the youngest drug and alcohol addicted kids in the city.

I lost track of her when she ran away. I saw her once or twice in forty years. When she heard through the grapevine what happened to Jessie, she reached out to me on Facebook and we reconnected.

What an incredible story of survival and triumph hers is. She now speaks throughout the Midwest for organizations such as Exploit No More, Celebrate Recovery, and Milwaukee's Anti-Trafficking Task Force.

Barbie's text said: *Jesus Calling. Keep your eyes on Me! Waves of adversity are washing over you, and you feel tempted to give up. As your circumstances consume more and more of your attention, you are losing sight of Me. Yet, I am with you always, holding you by your right hand. I am fully aware of your situation, and I will not allow you to be tempted beyond what you are able to bear.*

I was not only dealing with Jessie's loss, but also the loss of one of my brothers. We hadn't spoken in four months since a devastating blow up on my back patio. It was the worst argument I have ever had with anyone. Plus, I had lost my best non-human friend, Milo, our ten-year-old lab, and also my ability to run, my life's passion, the year before Jess died. On top of all that, I was dealing with a painful private matter that fit Barbie's "temptation" text to a tee. It had to do with my second question. *What do I do about R?*

135

I was feeling like Job.

Where did that come from? I texted back.
Barbie wrote: *A book I'm reading called* Jesus Calling.
Me: *Wow, how did you know how perfect that was for me today?*
Barbie: *I didn't. Something just told me to send it to you.*

Two weeks later, a beautiful, rich brown, leather-bound book was waiting in a box. FedEx had dropped it at the front door. It was from Barbie: *Jesus Calling.*

I have read, used, and absorbed to the best of my ability the devotionals in this book every day since. They are among the most practical and transformative lessons I've learned, and I've done a lot of personal growth seminars. Just another resource, aptly introduced, at the perfect time, when it was most needed, when I was most open to it, heating, hammering, shaping, and molding this hard, rough metal a little further into something ever more useful.

February became March. Ever so slowly, I was moving through the darkness, making progress. But just as the Wisconsin winter was advancing, but far from yielding to spring, I was still far from emerging.

f Buck Blodgett
March 22, 2014

Happy BDay, Jess.

Twenty years ago today. A new soul born into this world. Brightened it forever. The most magical, memorable day of my life. I'll never forget when that little purple head came out, eyes wide open, no hospital, no drugs, just you, needing nothing but love. Those eyes stayed wide open for nineteen years. First thirteen, you soaked in all you could of our world. Last six, you began to comment on it, and purposefully and intentionally shine your beaming light out into it with all you had. So proud of you. So blessed to have nineteen years with you. My best friend (with Mom). The button on your purse said, "In this world to change this world." You meant it. LOVE YOU FOREVER my angel. LOVE>hate.

chapter thirty-four

THE TALENT SHOW

"Close your eyes, sing out loud,
Just forget the world, and the crowd.
I know you're scared of 'em,
But you'll learn to love 'em, yeah."

—Jessie Blodgett, "Butterflies"

MY PHONE RANG ONE DAY back in Black February, a month earlier. It was Sheila Parker from Jessie's high school.

I remembered Ms. Parker. She ran the talent show every year. Jessie participated in a lot of co-curriculars in high school, like Forensics, State Solo & Ensemble, the plays and musicals, Philosophy Club, Chess Club, to name a few. But the talent show was her time to shine, her favorite of all the events in high school, and the thing she was most proud of.

Ms. Parker said, "Every year the HUHS Talent Show selects a charity of choice and raises about a thousand dollars. This year, we'd like to donate our proceeds to Jessie's Memorial Fund. Would that be okay?

"We'd also like to invite your family to the two shows as our guests of honor, and do a tribute to Jess, if that's okay…."

I felt the amazing Great OKness again.

Ms. Parker continued. "The talent show has always been in February, but we had conflicts this year, so we scheduled it for Friday, March 21 and Saturday, March 22. Will that weekend work?"

"Sheila," I said, "Did you know that March 22 is Jessie's birthday?"

Silence.

"Oh, my gosh, no, I didn't know that."

I could hear her thinking. *Is this good? Will they need privacy to grieve? What should I say now?*

"Those dates would be perfect. I don't know what to say…. Thanks. We'd be honored to be there."

Not only was the twenty-second of March Jessie's birthday, but the twenty-first was her grandpa's birthday. Her grandpa, my dad, bought Jess her first piano and got her started in music.

Grandpa came for opening night of the 2014 HUHS Talent Show, just as he had done the four years when Jess was in it. It was his eighty-fourth birthday. We almost lost my dad nineteen years earlier when he had a heart attack and a double bypass. Jessie was a year old then. But he survived, lived to see his grandchildren grow up, and had now outlived one of them. Grandpa rarely missed one of her musical performances.

Other family and friends came too. Ms. Parker saved two sections for us. It was a bittersweet trip down memory lane, especially for my mom (Grammie to Jess), and my sister, Becky.

Sheila Parker walked out on stage. A spotlight lit the darkness and fell on her. A hush fell over the crowd.

"Welcome, everyone, to the 2014 Hartford Union High School Talent Show. Two years ago, the Student Council had to drop its sponsorship. A core group of dedicated students came to me and pleaded for the survival of their treasured event. Their leadership saved it. One of those students was Jessie Blodgett.

"As you all know, Jessie was taken from us last year. Tonight, we remember her."

A few quiet sobs broke the silent darkness around us.

"Jessie was a fixture in our show for four years. As a freshman in 2009, with thirty-five competitors, she won third place for her original piece 'Butterflies.' As a sophomore in 2010, together with Tyler Sandblom, she won second place and brought the house down with their rendition of the Jason Mraz and Colby Callait hit duet, 'Lucky.' As a junior and a senior, Jessie won first place in the Best Original Artist category. And those of us who were there will never forget her belting out Adelle's 'Rolling in the Deep.'

"Please join me and all of our performers tonight in welcoming the Blodgett family, remembering Jessie, and dedicating our show to her."

The thundering applause warmed my heart and brought, once more, the overwhelming perfect peace.

The room went black again. The spotlight fell on the MC, as she walked on stage. It was Jackie, Jessie's best friend.

It was Jess who encouraged Jackie to participate in Forensics, in the HUHS Talent Shows, and in life. Jackie called Jessie not just her best friend, but her big sister and her role model.

Jackie didn't know the show would be dedicated to Jess when she signed on as MC, and Sheila Parker didn't know they were best friends when she recruited Jackie. To top it off, one of the entries had to scratch on Friday. On the spur of the moment, Jackie and her brother Aaron filled the vacant spot.

They did their comedy Forensics piece and performed their hearts out.

Competing against two-dozen other acts, they won.

On the way out, in the lobby, someone called my name.

"Hey, Mr. Blodgett!"

It was one of the young performers, a freshman I think. She had done a modern dance interpretation piece. It was the kind of performance that the teenage Buck—the wanna be cocky tough guy who was into sports and had no appreciation of the arts—would have judged. I would have thought it was weird. I would have thought she wasn't cool."

But I was being worked on now, being forged in the fire, hammered, shaped, and molded. My eyes were being renewed by One greater than me and you. And what they saw was the courage in this young person—a free spirit, with no fear of her own unique artistic expression, and no fear of the judgments of people like me. Suddenly I was not superior to her, but in awe of her. I knew I could never do what she just did.

And then she said, "Jessie was my voice teacher. Remember me? I came to your house! She taught me how to sing. She taught me to never be afraid to be myself."

141

I felt a strange mixture of shame for my judgments and gratitude for my new eyes and for the gift she had just given me. I told her what a beautiful performance she gave. Her face lit up in a beaming proud smile, and off she ran, before I could tell her how much I admired her.

And then it was March 22, 2014. This was a dark, dark day for Joy. She tried to focus on being grateful for the nineteen years we had with Jess. But it was no use. It was too soon. There would be no peace, happy memories, and gratitude for Joy today. Just the overwhelming pain. She would cry again today, as she had every day since July 15, only more.

The following day Laura Gruber took another message from Jessie:

Tell my dad I had the BEST birthday ever! J
So many beautiful gifts.
All the love from all of you—right back at you.

Jackie would later tell me that when she stepped on stage that night she felt Jess's presence so strongly it almost distracted her. I felt it, too. Was she really there? My soul knew the answer, but my mind still had trouble believing.

How happy Jess must have been, seeing the HUHS Talent Show dedicated to her, on her birthday, with her best friend as MC, and proceeds donated to her project to end male on female violence and add Love to our world.

Then to see Jackie and Aaron win it, and dedicate their win to her....

chapter thirty-five

CARRY ON MY WAYWARD SON

"'Cause you'll be searching the whole world 'round..."
—Jessie Blodgett, "Music"

MOST OF THIS BOOK IS about the miracles, the events that transpired after our tragedy that changed me, compelled me to bear witness and share with the world the string of occurrences that spoke of the Divine.

Of course, most of life—the mundane minutes and moments—was just normal life. But life would never be normal again. No, it would be a moment-to-moment wrestling match, a constant duel for my attention between the abyss and the life of purpose.

It would have been easy to get sucked into the sadness, to just go there and stay. Some days it felt like Joy and I could give up and walk right off the edge. What did we have left to live for anyway? Our only child was gone, and with her our hopes for her future, and for ours, for grandchildren. We were alone and aging before our time.

On April Fools' Day, Laura Gruber and I met again at my new home away from home, the Perc Place. On my way in, though I really didn't have to go, I stopped in the bathroom, just to read the walls. *Everyone has a photographic memory; some of us just don't have film.* Unfortunately, I could totally relate. I understand now that brain fog comes with stress and depression.

I was excited about meeting with Laura again. It seemed like our first meeting on January 31 was so long ago. She gave me the first message then, and the skeptic in me formulated those three test questions.

I believed the first question was answered. *How many minutes did it take you to die?* Through Monica's medium, Jess said, "2." Then, Laura had said the answer was "yes" to something…. The fourth question, the one that felt given to me: *Will I see you again?*

But since that time, I had no more answers. What about the other two?

I'd been given so much more than I ever imagined possible since that first night in the hotel room after Jessie's killing. The Great OKness brought peace beyond understanding to my bleeding heart that night, and many times since.

But the more time passed without confirmation of my questions, the more doubt grew.

Out of the bathroom now and sipping on a London Fog (English tea infused with cream, you should really try one), Laura shared with me the whole message she received two days after the Talent Show:

Tell my dad I had the BEST birthday ever! J. So many beautiful gifts. All the love from all of you—right back at you. You

all rock! My dad is the best—I am very proud of him. Thanks for the butterfly kisses—song Butterflies are free to fly, fly away, fly high (I know you'll look it up) haha! I am always around. Look for me.... I always need to remind my parents that I did **NOT** leave them and never will. Dan chose to leave but I did not (67). I just moved to a new level of spiritual love. I will physically see you all again (or you me), but I want you to close your eyes and see me, then really feel my presence, for I am always there. LOVE>hate, oh, how true it is. Dad, save the children. I am sooooo proud of you. I love you so much. Carry on my wayward son. There'll be peace when you are done.

(Look it up, Laura)

J,

Bye

Nothing.

No answer to: *What should I do about R?* No answer to: *What does God want me to do next?* Completely absent was any new amazing thing Jess said that only I could know.

I read it again. There were some profound, if true, and curious things in there. What was that (67) doing in the middle? When I first read it, I glanced up at Laura. She gave me a questioning look. Obviously, we were both puzzled.

What about the reference to the Kansas and Elton John songs? Well, "Carry on My Wayward Son" was interesting, as it was one of my favorite songs as a teenager, one that we listened to regularly back in the seventies. Same with the Elton John song. Laura had brought copies of the lyrics to both tunes.

Laura and I always left our meetings energized. She was my connection to Jess. And I was her proof that her gift was real. But, though we both understood sometimes one had to wait for the unfolding, we left deflated. Again.

For the next forty-eight hours, I looked for 67s everywhere. License plates. Billboards. TV. Radio. Mail. Facebook. Bills. Everywhere. I violated every rule of objectivity. I searched high and low. I could not find one single 67 for two days. Nor was there any sign of answers to my other two test questions.

And the doubt grew.

"67"

"Don't say you can't, you'll be alright…"
—Jessie Blodgett, "Overnight"

A FEW DAYS BACK, I had texted Aaron (he won the talent show with Jackie): *Can we get together soon and work on the resolution again?*

Aaron had replied: *I don't know how to fix it. I'm stuck. But sure. I can meet you in the library at the high school during Resource, my last study hour, on Thursday.*

Aaron was helping me create and refine the video I had shown Pastor John, The LOVE>hate Project Trailer. Aaron knew how to use Windows Movie Maker, and he taught me.

While the video was powerful, according to friends, family, and Pastor John, who said, "Get ready…" it needed technical help. The resolution was bad. It wouldn't work for presenting on a big screen. This was our plan, to present to high schools all over the country. But we were stuck. My lack of tech skills compounded my anxiety.

Entering the high school to meet Aaron was emotional—a flash-back. The last time I was in the library was with Jessie. To get there, I had to negotiate a corridor full of hundreds of energized high school students hustling to their next classes and packing in social time every second along the way, as only teenagers can.

They were so alive.

And Jess was so *not* alive.

I could almost see her laughing and bouncing down the halls with her friends.

Still, it felt good to be back in her stomping grounds.

I worked my way to the back of the library, where Aaron was sitting with friends.

"Hi, Buck!"

"Hey, Aaron. You ready to try?"

"Yeah, for sure, but I don't know…. I've already tried, like, a bunch of times."

My heart sank a little further.

I should have known better by now—that obstacles, barriers and "the impossible" were no match for Providence. They were just enrichment devices used to reveal the complex orchestrations of the Great Artist, to inspire awe, faith, and growth.

But I remain human.

My human intellect gets in the way of my soul, like a fog that lifts briefly but then descends even thicker. Like an eclipse when the moon blots out the sun.

Just then, Aaron called out, "Hey! Lucas!"

As Lucas walked over, Aaron explained quickly that Lucas was the resident movie maker guru and all around computer genius. Aaron had asked him to help us.

"Lucas, Buck made a video for his project, but we can't get the resolution right. He can't use the video for his big screen presentations."

Lucas reeled off some instructions and took me to a place in my computer I've never been. To this day, I have no idea what he had me do, or how to get back there should I need to.

We arrived at a screen with a bunch of set up options and drop down choices and numbers on it.

Lucas said, "That's it. Click on that!"

So I did. A number came up. Thirty-nine. Thirty-nine what? I couldn't tell you; I have no idea what it meant.

"Click and hold on that, all the way up, as far as it goes," Lucas said.

The numbers raced up and stopped at their max.

Sixty-seven.

Lucas and Aaron both frowned. They were looking for a big number, like a thousand or something.

"Hmm, that's not gonna do it," Lucas said. My radar was up: 67. There it was.

Lucas said, "Click out of there, let's just look at it and see what it's like now."

We went back to my video. I clicked play. The resolution was perfect.

"Oh, wow," Lucas and Aaron said together, surprised. "It worked."

Lucas led me somewhere else. I can't tell you where. I just surrendered to his expertise.

"Okay, now click download."

The download bar was moving very slowly: …1%…2%…3%. I could tell it was going to be awhile. I rested my mind and let the boys talk.

After a full two minutes, I turned back to my laptop: 67%. Almost as if to highlight, the download stuck on 67% for several long seconds, then jumped instantly to 100%. Done!

No way! I could not find a 67 for two whole days. Now I found two in two minutes. Or they found me. The fact didn't escape me that the two 67s were not just on some random billboard, license plate, TV show, or Facebook post.

No, they occurred immediately and spontaneously after the solving of our obstacle, our "impossible," when the video, the cornerstone of our message LOVE>hate, was perfected and finished.

Like with so many things, I did not fully understand what just happened. In the coming months, I would see how impactful this video was. I would come to understand that 67 meant this: Help will always be available, and there is no obstacle to our work that could stop it. I am with you always. Have a little faith.

I left the high school ecstatic and infused once again with hope and purpose.

But within minutes, I would get a third 67…. One that would pull me right back into darkness. This was nuts. I couldn't go on like this. When did I become a drama king? (I'll explain this 67 shortly.)

chapter thirty-seven

PROOF OF HEAVEN

"So hold my hand and watch me
Fall into the sky..."
—Jessie Blodgett, "Butterflies"

AFTER MY DAY OF 67S, of ups and downs, my head hit the pillow hard. I was dog tired, running on fumes, but also wired and troubled. I would need to read to get to sleep.

I reached for *Proof of Heaven*, a book I had borrowed from a local support group for people who lost loved ones. It was about a near death experience (NDE), the third such book I read that month or ever, for that matter.

The story was reaching its climax. It was compelling nonfiction written by a neurosurgeon that contracted bacterial meningitis. The bacteria had literally eaten away ninety percent of his brain. They had the imaging to prove it.

He could not have survived. No one had previously survived such a severe case of meningitis according to his neurosurgeon colleagues. But he made a complete and miraculous recovery.

But that wasn't the cool part. Upon waking from his week-long coma, he told the story of where he was: Heaven. He described his out of body journey in rich and vivid detail. He reported colors and music far more vibrant and alive than we could possibly imagine from our world, and other such things commonly reported in NDE cases.

But the compelling part of his story, to the biologist and doctor in me, was his convincing argument that it was not possible for his physical brain to dream or imagine this amazing experience he had while in a coma—because ninety percent of his cerebral cortex was destroyed.

This is the region of the human brain responsible for higher thought, imagination, and conceptualization. It was physically impossible for his nonfunctional cerebral cortex to dream the vivid dreams he had. His explanation for this experience was that it was real, and his consciousness had actually traveled away from his physical body.

Near the end of the book, there was a long poem. The poem was good, but the book was working—drowsiness was taking me. I was close to marking the page and rolling over, as my mind was slipping into No Man's Land. Suddenly, I got the feeling Jessie was using the poem to talk to me.

Stimulated again, I read on. Every word of the poem seemed to somehow fit. Either it was something Jess said to me, or something I said to her, or something that fit her outlook on life, or our situation since she had passed. The further I read, the more perfect every word.

153

And then the deep peace washed through me again. Finishing the last sentence on the page, somehow I knew…. My eyes went to the page number in the upper right corner—one hundred and sixty-seven.

P.S. The author, the comatose neurosurgeon, described being escorted through Heaven "on the wings of a giant butterfly."

The next day, I texted Laura Gruber about the 67s. She was as excited as I was. We scheduled coffee for the following Thursday.

Joy and I walked into the Perc Place together that day, April 10, 2014—my fifty-fourth birthday—to meet Laura and her daughter, Emily. I was pleased Joy was joining us, and so were the Grubers. She had not been overly enthused with all these crazy signs and messages I kept telling her about. I just wanted her to meet Laura. Plus, we didn't get out together enough.

I wasn't looking forward to my birthday, my first without Jess. Every special day now was darkened by her absence. I was glad to be spending part of this day with Joy and the Gruber girls.

We sat down. Laura and Emily were grinning from ear to ear.

"What?" I said.

"Well, we have something else to tell you. Go ahead, Emily."

Emily started. "Well, Mom called me a half hour ago and said, 'Hey, it's Buck's birthday. Can you stop at Walmart and pick up two birthday cards, one from each of us?'"

I thought they were about to do something for my birthday, and I got a little embarrassed. I didn't like attention in public places.

Emily continued. "Driving to Walmart, I popped in the CD of uplifting songs you burned for Mom last month. 'I Hope You Dance,' by Leann Womack, was playing."

I knew the song and the tune played in my head.

"I pulled into the lot. I was running a little late, so when I parked I said a quick prayer and asked for help finding two perfect cards fast."

Emily and Laura Gruber were a little further along at this relationship with a Higher Power thing than I was.

"Right away, I found a nice card with a big monarch butterfly on it. Perfect. That was one. Then I went to the musical cards section. I'm not sure why. I hate those cards. Usually they're all wiener dogs and dumb ditties. I looked at several cards. Yup. All wiener dogs and dumb ditties. I was about to leave that section when I picked up one last card. When I opened it, it played, 'I Hope You Dance,' by Leann Womack."

Emily took a big breath and went on. "Well, that caught my attention. Weird, the song from the car.

"Then on my way to check out, I happened to glance at the barcodes on both cards. Not sure why I did that either."

Emily handed me the two birthday cards, smiling expectantly. I took my time reading them, letting in their "Happy Birthday" messages. Then I read the barcodes. Both started with the number 67.

Emily jumped back in. "Even though I was late for getting here, I had to run back to the card section. I checked about ten other cards around those two. None of them had barcodes that started with 67."

155

Sometime after all the 67s that week, I looked back at the March 24 dictation Laura received from Jess.

I saw that whole message in a different light. All these timely 67s now lent some validity to the message as a whole. I saw the meaning in the songs by Elton John and Kansas.

The Kansas song was for me…there'll be peace when I am done.

But the Elton John song, well, call me a grieving dad searching for comfort whose imagination was running wild—part of me agrees with you. But for that other part of me, this was the long awaited answer to my revised first question.

How many minutes did it take for you to die, sweetie? You see, as the days had passed with no answer, it ate at me, and I revised it to: *What do YOU want me to know about the process of your passing?*

Was this what Jess wanted me to know, these lyrics from the Elton John song? (Look them up.) That someone saved her life…? She was rescued when she was roped and tied…? From a slip noose in her darkest dreams…? Sweet freedom whispered in her ear, set her free to fly away, high away? Butterflies are free to fly?

My mind raced. The comatose neurosurgeon in *Proof of Heaven* flew on the wings of a butterfly. Laura's first message from Jess said: *…Butterflies everywhere, Dad; I'll share them with you.*

Dr. Karl had told his wife he was sending a giant monarch to carry her away from the pain. She sunk into peace and died in his arms.

Back in January, a patient brought in an article. It stated the butterfly predated Christianity as a symbol for life after death, and was, along with the cross itself, one of the oldest Christian symbols of the resurrection. It also included testimonials of ADCs (after-death communications) stating the butterfly was the most commonly reported sign.

And, of course, Jess had written her first song, "Butterflies," which contained the lyrics: *"Hold my hand and watch me fall into the sky,"* and *"Butterflies…fly free…fly free."*

The layers kept building.

I envisioned an angel coming to Jess in her darkest hour, her horrible pain and terror. As the rope bit hard into her neck, cutting off her air, the grip too hopelessly strong for her to fight off, as she began to get dizzy and the carbon dioxide pounded inside her head and lungs, as she fought desperately, bewildered by the betrayal and cruelty of a friend, the angel came to save her. Out of her body it called her soul. Floating up and away together the angel whispered in her ear, "Fly away, fly high. You're a butterfly, and butterflies are free to fly…."

R

"But in the end there's you and there's me…
Something that must never be."
—Jessie Blodgett/Ian Nytes, "Love by Proxy"

WHAT SHOULD I DO ABOUT R?

It was late April when R and I exchanged our final texts. (R was really her nickname.)

She was a patient in our clinic. R was younger, full of life, kind. R lost her soul mate and best friend a few months before Jess passed. We had profound loss and deep sadness in common. She had also known violence up close.

At first, it was the same deep connection I shared with many of my favorite patients. Chiropractors are blessed to have long-term trusting relationships with patients, and though it is important to maintain professionalism, sometimes a select few will become friends, like Hans.

That growing connection between R and me was my fault. I was breaking all the rules. Through twenty-nine years of marriage and eighteen years in practice, I had developed, like doctors and husbands are supposed to, a keen awareness of boundaries, and an internal discipline for not crossing them. But when Jess was killed so violently, so shockingly, I knew that I must not get bitter and close down.

I responded by opening my heart wide, by speaking and living that Love is greater than hate. I became far more outgoing, more understanding, and less judgmental. I lived aware of the preciousness of every second of life. I felt high all the time. I felt raw and broken, but strong; profoundly sad and vulnerable, yet resilient; heartbroken but watched over by a Higher Power—all at the same time.

I made many new friends, and spent more time with old ones. I hugged everybody every day, family, friends, staff, and patients, and told them I loved them.

Like Dana and I—we now hugged and said "I love you" every time we got together. I did this with everyone. My three best friends Mark, Dave, and Hans—we often shed tears when we talked now, and they were guys' guys. Cultural rules were being pushed aside, shackles were breaking, grown men were hugging and saying "I love you." It was sweet. It was freeing.

R came in one day and, out of the blue, said, "I can't come anymore."

"What do you mean? Why not?"

"We got too close. And the kids (her beautiful young children) are getting too attached to you."

At the time, I thought it was fine. I was letting my love out with everyone in my life. Jessie's murder had cut me to the core, and I now believed that I was here to Love as fully as I could every single day, and I no longer cared about rules and laws and culture that told us to withhold our Love. Plus, I trusted myself to do the right thing and never cross boundaries, which I had always done. I actually thought R might be a little crazy, the kind of person that imagines things differently than they actually are.

R said she needed to say goodbye to the staff, to explain this would be her last visit, because they had become friends.

"What do you want me to tell them?" she asked.

"Whatever you need to," I said.

I didn't feel I should tell her what to say. I didn't even realize she needed to separate herself until she mentioned it. We had done nothing wrong. We never held hands, kissed, had sex, or even sexted, met outside of the clinic, or had any inappropriate contact while alone in the treatment rooms beyond typical chiropractic care.

I tried to tell R that maybe our feelings and perceptions were a little different, but what we do about those feelings—our actions— were what counted. We could maintain a professional relationship with clear boundaries.

Looking back, maybe I argued too hard.

She insisted that we were too close and she had to leave. So she did. We said a sad goodbye.

After I finished with the cluster of patients that followed, I went up to the front desk area. I immediately noticed that the energy was weird. My staff was avoiding my eyes.

"What? What did R say?" I said.

"She told us you two were in love and she had to leave."

What?! I wasn't in love with her. Falling in love with a patient is a major no-no in health care. I was shocked and angry.

I explained everything from my point of view to Chris, Mel, Kim, and Holly. After all, they were my work family. They'd seen my worst days and understood. Losing their trust and respect would have been another gut punch to my wounded faith in life.

I have never had a problem with a patient that I didn't ultimately resolve, and I didn't want her experience in our clinic, and our friendship, to end like this. Deep down, we had a connection through tragedy, and I wanted to preserve it and be loyal too.

Even at my age, I can be thick and naïve. It took several weeks of texting to clear the air, to understand she really did love me. I know that sounds stupid, but I have a history of low self-esteem, and I thought she was out of my league. I didn't see what she saw in me, that she didn't want anything and wasn't trying to cause trouble; she just loved me. When that finally dawned on me, something inside snapped, and I suddenly developed strong feelings. I let myself go somewhere mentally that I had never been. I began to imagine what it would be like to be together.

It was wrong. I knew it. She knew it. Over the next several months, we'd stop texting for a month or more, only to start up for a day or two again. After a few bouts of that, we stopped for good.

I was in the depths of despair that second coldest Wisconsin winter on record. I had lost Jessie, the light of my life. I had let myself mentally go somewhere so wrong. I was drowning in guilt that I hurt over R, when all of my pain should have been for Jess and for Joy. I had also lost my brother, my dog, and my passion—running. I was lost and depressed, a failure as a dad and as a husband.

I knew I needed to tell Joy everything.

And I did.

Joy already knew about R. I had told her months earlier, right after R announced her feelings to the staff.

And now, I told her again…the rest of the story.

My beautiful wife understood.

She understood the intense raw need in me to fill the massive hole in my heart. She understood the appeal to start over with a new family with young children, having lost my only child and the chance for grandkids. Joy understood the loneliness of grief, and the mechanism behind the deeper connections I was making with others. She saw that R and I were like magnets being pulled to one another, not conscious of the science behind what was happening, just caught in the pull.

Joy and I shared our honest feelings, all of them, good and bad, right and wrong. We shared our struggles and pain over this. And then we re-committed to keep communicating honestly and deeply, forever.

I tried to stay focused on Jess, Joy, and God throughout that winter. The signs kept coming—the sound from Jessie's bedroom light, the chimes, the messages from Laura, the 67s, *Jesus Calling* with His timely lesson that He wouldn't let me be tempted beyond what I could bear. But the pain and emptiness were always there, too, waiting for the latest sign to fade so they could surface once more and lay waste to hope.

When I left the high school back on February 3, right after Aaron and Lucas fixed the resolution on the video, right after two 67s found me in two minutes, I got a text. It was R. It had been weeks since our last contact.

I know we said no more…but I'm going under in ten minutes, and I just needed to tell you.

I was heartbroken, and sick with myself.

What do you mean? You're going under?

162

R: *I'm having major surgery and they're about to put me out.*

Me: *I'm in Hartford. I just left the high school. I'll come right now. Where are you? I just have to call Joy first and tell her.*

R: *I'm at the hospital, on Highway 67.*

He was in *every* aspect of my life, even the wrong parts. He was everywhere, always, and He was helping me, teaching me, getting me through the pain, showing me the path, not condemning me but honoring my weakness and using it.

That would have been the first time R and I met anywhere other than my clinic. I called Joy, expecting her to understand and trust me. She never had a reason not to. I knew she wouldn't like it, but…R was alone in her time of need.

Joy surprised me and said, "No."

I told you that I was thick and naïve sometimes, and, of course humanly selfish and needy too. I argued that I was trustworthy and had the right to stand by a friend. Joy refused to be okay with this. Her instincts told her I wasn't in control of this situation, and going to R's side during surgery would pull her closer.

Now I had to call R before she went under and tell her I wasn't coming. She'd have to go through major surgery alone.

I think about her sometimes. I wonder how this could have happened. How could I have let this happen? I get mad at myself. I get mad at God. How could He have let this happen? (As if it were His fault.) Didn't I have enough pain and loss? Didn't Joy have enough pain and loss?

Then I remember what someone once said to me: God doesn't make bad things happen; He uses them and turns them to good, if you ask Him.

R once said that she would haunt me for years. It sounded a little crazy at the time, but she was right.

As I have said to Joy, to R, to Jessie, and to my Creator many times: I remain one hundred percent committed to my wife. I am proud that I have never been physically unfaithful in my marriage. But I have been mentally weak, and tempted....

For letting myself go where I did, and for this chapter of my book and of my life—honey, Joy, I am so very sorry.

THE SECOND QUESTION

---

*"Every question has an answer
...Just around the river bend."*
—Jessie Blodgett, "Overnight"

THE SECOND EMAIL LAURA GRUBER ever sent, the day after I met her, was about an episode of the *Dr. Oz Show* featuring Spiritual Medium Rebecca Rosen. She had a book, *Awaken the Spirit Within,* which Laura insisted I read.

I never watched the show. I meant to, but I had been fighting despair and was increasingly busy running a clinic full-time and laying all the groundwork for The LOVE>hate Project. I was doing a lot of writing and meeting with a lot of people. I was also being given all kinds of books, links, and other resources to check out about violence against women. I just didn't have the time to read or watch everything people were sending. Laura's recommendation disappeared into the past.

Several weeks later, over coffee at the Perc Place, Laura asked if I had a chance to watch that Dr. Oz episode.

I told her no.

She was excited nonetheless. She had begun reading *Awaken the Spirit Within*. And she had purchased an extra copy for me. I told her thanks. I would get to it at some point….

"If it's not the right time, it's not the right time," she said. "I'll hang onto it until you're ready."

Laura was ahead of me in understanding Divine timing.

During another get-together at the Perc Place, now in late March, Laura asked again if I was ready for the book.

I was nearing the end of *Proof of Heaven*, so I said yes. *Awaken the Spirit Within* became my next bedtime read.

About a week later, I crawled under the covers and kissed Joy goodnight. We chatted for a minute, then I popped in my earplugs and flipped on the soft nightstand lamp. I picked up the book again, as Joy lay watching TV next to me.

Awaken the Spirit Within was divided into three sections. Parts One and Three were small, only about twenty-some pages each. The bulk of the book was Part Two—well over two hundred pages. It contained ten chapters, the ten steps to ignite your spiritual life and fulfill your divine purpose.

I opened the book, flipped to my bookmark at the end of Part One…and turned the page. Page twenty-six was different from every other page in the book. It had just one paragraph:

166

THE SIGNIFICANCE
OF THE LETTER

R

*Each step of your awakening begins with the letter R.
In Hebrew, this letter is pronounced "resh" and it
begins the Hebrew word Ruach ha-kadosh, which
roughly translated means "Holy Spirit." According to
early mystical Judaic literature, when the letter R, or
"resh," is chanted or meditated on, it is believed to
awaken our spiritual senses and open us up to
spiritual insights, guidance, truth, and transcendence.*

I missed it at first. I missed that big capital "R," the biggest letter
in the whole book. In fact, I got distracted by an upwelling of
sadness, and caught myself thinking of R again. I realized my brain
and heart had been triggered by this big letter.

And then it hit me.

It hit me like a lightning bolt. It hit me like a spiritual shockwave.
Oh…my…God.

I re-read the paragraph below the big capital R at warp speed,
senses heightened. Then, I flipped back to the Table of Contents to
check on something. Yes! The titles of the ten chapters, the ten steps
to ignite your spiritual life and fulfill your divine purpose:

Reflect
Reset
Recognize Your Role
Reside in Love

Release and Reenergize
Rejoice in Gratitude
Rest Assured
Relinquish Control
Reclaim Your Power
Rise Up

My mind reeled. This was the answer to my second question: *What should I do about R?*

Just like the first question, after days without an answer, I had also revised the second question: *Just give me an R.* That would be sign enough.

Here it was. My R—a big, bold, capital R. An R that was sacred and began the ancient Hebrew word meaning Holy Spirit. An R that was believed to open us up to spiritual insights, guidance, and truth.

And there wasn't just one, but a whole book full of them. All of them pointing me in a direction, toward spiritual awakening and divine purpose. All of them telling me exactly "what to do about R," step-by-step.

Never again would I think of R and not simultaneously think of God, because, in Hebrew, that's basically what it meant. In other words, when my mind, in its human weakness, went to a wrong place, a place that could be harmful to me and others, there was now a trigger in place that would instantly aim it back toward the *right* place.

The Great Artist did not make bad things happen to me. But when I brought them on myself, and suffered the pain of having done so, when I let my mind go in weakness where I should not have and fell for another woman when I was already in love with and committed to Joy, still He was there. He was always there, finding another way to use my pain and my problem to draw me closer.

I could barely wait to call Laura the next day and tell her about the Rs. I didn't tell her until several months later that R was a person. But she got it anyway—how the Grand Designer had taken a simple request and responded with an avalanche of Rs, wove them into religious history and spiritual instruction, answered my question (both versions), and also *gave me the tools* to handle my problem.

Wow! Now *that* was an answer.

Laura was chuckling.

"Buck, I think you missed a couple things. Remember who the author is?"

Rebecca Rosen. R.R. A line from *Bruce Almighty* came to mind, when Jim Carrey said to God, *"Now you're just showing off!"*

I was back in that peace-beyond-understanding state of grace and gratitude again, pondering the two-and-a-half-month wait for this answer, with all the times of doubt. And then the explosion of an answer so overflowing it left no doubt.

Laura said, "Buck, do you remember when I first sent you that email? Look it up."

I did. February first.

Within twenty-four hours of getting Jessie's first message from Laura and devising my test questions, I received the answer to the second one. It just took two and a half months for me to be ready for it. Unbelievable.

Who is this Creator? How could He navigate time and circumstance in all its complexity to arrange for that show to be aired when it was? And for Laura, who knew nothing of it's *real* significance to me, to see it and tell me about it?

Throw in all the 67s, the butterfly signs, the holiday happenings, and messages from Jess. The layers upon layers kept building.

And then multiply that by seven billion people on our planet. Was He doing this with everyone all the time? Do most just miss it all because their eyes are not open? The amazing, mind-blowing complexity of the universal tapestry left me feeling small. I felt like a character in a video game, and He was the super genius Game King, orchestrating the lives of billions. But the game was real, and the game was Love in Action. Truly awesome He was.

The compounding intricacy of the Great Weaver's web was shaping me. One could only be humbled by such talent, beauty, and power. And I was. This was another gift. Humility is a core ingredient, along with gratitude and trust, for receiving His amazing Love, because it's never forced on us. So, the more He blew me away with His orchestrations, the more He blessed me with humility, thereby enabling me to receive more effectively. It was a Holy vicious cycle.

In the days that followed, I reflected on the test questions I had asked. It was still difficult to believe from inside The Game here on planet earth.

1. It took Jess 2 minutes to pass.
2. I had been given guidance in an avalanche of Rs.
4. Yes, we would meet again.

But question three remained unanswered: *What does God want me to do next?*

Looking back, two significant events occurred in the weeks following that question. First: Barbie sent me *Jesus Calling*. I have used it every day since. It's developing my ability to hear the Voice. Second: I met with Jessie's friend, Somer, and her mom, Terri, who sparked my idea for the trailer.

That was what I should do next—draw closer to Him every day, and make a video that would move people.

I haven't met with Somer or her mom since. Sometimes the Game King brings people into our lives to stay; other times they drop in for a brief encounter, contribute their gift, message, or lesson, and then go on their merry way.

It took me three months to see that all my questions had been answered back in Black February. Sometimes our prayers have already been answered, and our needs met. He is patiently waiting for us to get up to speed.

Contained in one of Laura's messages from Jess was a reference to "just around the river bend" from Pocahontas, the Disney movie that spurred Jessie's love of nature as a child. She included that phrase in her second song way back in seventh grade. *"Every question has an answer…just around the river bend."*

Driving home one day, listening to Jessie's CD, it dawned on me: every question most certainly did have an answer, now that I had eyes to see and ears to hear.

So what lessons have I learned from my test questions, the 67s, and this whole R thing?

Well, quite a few. I have learned you can call supernatural phenomena coincidence, but you would have to ignore incalculable probabilities, and you would have to rationalize the inexplicable, nonsensical feelings of profound peace, comfort, and Love that consistently accompany these coincidences.

I have learned when your heart is torn apart by terrible loss, if you open yourself up to it, Love will come from everywhere, everyone, and everything to help you heal.

I have learned when you resist the pull to close down after terrible loss, and instead open your heart wide, to everyone, life becomes extraordinary and even miraculous. But you have to watch out with that open heart. You have to police it better than I did, or you will hurt yourself and others, even if you don't mean to.

I have learned there are few things more valuable in this life than working through adversities with a loving and devoted wife. I have learned you can't help how you feel, but you can help what you do, and what choices you make.

I have learned Love is infinitely capable and strong. People have told me over and over this year how strong I am. Not true. I am no stronger than anyone else. In fact, I am quite weak, left to my own devices, as you now know. It is Love that is so strong, and that Love is available to all of us, always.

I have learned when I turn to Him for help, it will be given. It may not come *when* I want. It may not come *how* I want. I may not recognize it when it comes. But it will always be there. Even when I am not asking, it's there, waiting patiently for me to notice, never forcing itself. Because that's what Love does, even when I'm doing wrong.

I have learned I needed to be fully broken before I would fully surrender, thus inviting Him into my life. Now, I don't believe He caused the circumstances that broke me, but He was there waiting when they happened. Jessie's murder alone might not have been enough.... R, added to the loss of Jess, made me see how weak I was, and how deeply all of us crave Love, especially in times of great loss. *There is nothing and no one on earth that could fulfill the human longing for our Creator's Unconditional and Perfect Love.* It's a hard lesson, and I'm still learning it; I suspect I will be re-learning this one as long as I'm here, in one form or another. But I'm learning. I hope we all are.

And, finally, I have learned it's OK to be completely broken and imperfect. The Great Spirit likes us that way, for when the student is ready, the Master appears. It is from that broken place that we best access the Infinite.

MOTION TO SUPPRESS

"Be yourself…"
—Jessie Blodgett, "Butterflies"

I SHARED THESE SIGNS WITH Pastor John over coffee at the Perc Place. Rather than being put off by them, arguing against them, or quoting Bible verses to me, he listened intently. I even told him about R and *Awaken the Spirit Within*. You learn a lot about people when you tell them unusual things.

I shared another hurt I had. Someone thought I was "playing with the dark side." A friend had given me Bible verses warning me against talking with demons.

"Didn't I tell you?" Pastor John asked.

"Didn't you tell me what?"

"Didn't I tell you people were going to do that? Didn't I tell you when you took this unbelievable position, to Love and Forgive rather hate and seek vengeance? Didn't I tell you that you would encounter opposition and disbelief? Didn't I tell you some people would criticize and not understand? Even those closest to you?"

"What does the Bible say about communicating with lost loved ones, John? Was I only shown verses to support one side of the story? Is there another side?"

"Look," John said, "the Bible says this: God loves you, and He can and will do anything to let you know that. You are on a quest to bring Healing and Love and Forgiveness into this world. He is moving and inspiring you in amazing ways. Period. You must not let anyone or anything discourage you and stop the mission. You listen to God. That's it."

Isn't my pastor cool? I am blessed he fell into my life.

I am blessed by Ian, Amelia, and Aaron's presence in my life, as well. Ian built our website and recruited Amelia, his longtime girlfriend, to create a logo for The LOVE>hate Project. Ian's brother, Aaron, helped me make the video.

Amelia was creatively gifted, like most of Jessie's best friends. She designed an amazing logo. I was excited. We were official.

I loved Jessie's friends. This terrible tragedy made me appreciate them more, want to be around them more, want to help them through life more.

But, I thought to myself, we have a twenty-year-old designing our site, his little brother teaching me how to make videos, and his girlfriend designing our logo. Could we really pull this off?

We did.

On another day in April, I walked into Hartford Union High School looking for Principal Dobner. I didn't expect him to be available. He has fourteen hundred students and who knows how many faculty, parents, and federal regulations to worry about. But Brenda, his secretary, said, "Dan says come on in."

I showed Mr. Dobner the three-minute homespun video. I told him that I felt I was supposed to share Jessie's story—her life, her death, and her legacy—The LOVE>hate Project. I told him I was supposed to share it in schools, with young people, our future leaders. I explained that I had hoped to start in Hartford, see how it went, and then maybe take our message to other communities.

I asked Mr. Dobner, "Could I show this video and share my message at HUHS?"

"You bet you can. I'll look to see what class it would be most appropriate for."

"Well, actually, I don't want to talk to twenty kids in one class. I want to talk to every single kid in this school. Would it be possible to do a school-wide assembly?"

"Yes, yes it would."

"Could I have some tech support?"

"I'll have our Chief of Technology give you whatever you need."

"Could we have some expert counselors on hand available for any kids who are triggered by the presentation?"

"Yes, absolutely. Why don't you come back soon with your video. We'll show it to our counselors and make plans."

"Could we do it in October? What about on a Thursday?"

"Yes."

I met with Principal Dobner several times to plan and brainstorm. This is how all of our conversations went: I'd ask for something, he'd say yes to it all. Occasionally he'd add something like,

"Your message isn't just for high school students; the whole com-
munity needs to hear this. We should have a Community Event at
HUHS, too. I'll invite all the district principals from the other
Washington County high schools, plus counselors and the District
Administrator."

Back when we lived on Wayside Drive, Mr. Dobner was just a
neighbor. Jess and I would walk Mr. Milo, her 120-lb
lab/shepherd/golden mix, past his house and he'd always be out in
the yard playing with his kids. They'd wave to Mr. Milo, and us.

I knew I liked Dan Dobner back then.

And the help just kept coming.

Joy and I parked, once again, in the lot at the Washington County
Courthouse. It was April 18, 2014. Mom, Becky, Dana, Dad, and his
friend Pam were standing on the concrete sidewalk waiting for us.
We made our way through the big glass entranceway and up to the
shiny metal detectors.

"Hello there. How are you folks doing today? Empty pockets,
please. All metals in the tray." The stern faced security officers were
getting to know us now from our monthly appearances for hearings.

Working our way past security, through the glass doors and into
the wide tiled corridor to the first floor courtrooms, we saw the
defendant's clan gathered. They were waiting for the bailiff to open
the door to the courtroom.

It was always awkward to pass them. What were they thinking?
What were they feeling? Did they resent us for the position the
defendant was in, for the position his parents were in, for the position all of them were in for that matter?

"All rise."

Judge Martens entered the courtroom. Today he would rule on the Defense's motion to suppress, which they had entered at the last hearing back in March. I was nervous. This day had taken a long time to come.

In a nutshell, the motion to suppress was the Defense's contention that some evidence was improperly obtained, and that evidence should therefore be inadmissible in court. The evidence in question was the defendant's two interviews with police on the two days following Jessie's murder.

In his statement to Detective Thickens of the Hartford P.D. on Wednesday, July 17, the day after the Washington County Sheriff's Department called him while he was at our vigil, Dan was asked to account for his whereabouts at the time of Jessie's death.

Dan lied and said he was at his job.

When the police discovered Dan had never been employed at the place that he had claimed to work for the prior four months, they pressed him. Finally, he admitted to lying about work and stated that he was at Woodlawn Park in Hartford that Monday morning.

This led to the search of the park and the discovery of the cereal box containing the ligatures, tape, blood, hair, and wipes that the crime lab later discovered contained DNA from two people: Dan and Jessie.

If Dan had been improperly interviewed, if in any way his Miranda rights had been violated, if the Washington County Sheriff's Department, the Slinger P.D., or the Hartford P.D. had made any mistakes in processing or questioning him, then his statements in those two interviews could be ruled inadmissible. So could any evidence obtained as a result of his statements. The cereal box, the DNA evidence, and the bulk of the physical evidence that made this case "beyond a reasonable doubt" would all be thrown out, and with it the Prosecution's likelihood of being able to get a conviction.

Back on the courtroom benches, I sat with palms sweating.

Judge Martens began. "Mr. Bensen, Ms. Giernoth, it is the contention of the Defense that the defendant was improperly interviewed on July 16 and 17 of 2013. Furthermore, it is the Defense's contention that because of this, the defendant's rights were violated, and therefore his statements to police should not be considered by this court, nor should any evidence that those statements led to.

"Does the State have the video of the police interviews queued up?"

"Yes, we do, Your Honor."

"Please roll the video."

The courtroom was dead quiet. We would not see the videos in whole that day, or ever. We would only see the parts pertaining to Dan's processing. But those parts alone were riveting.

This was Dan the day after he had let himself into our house while Jess slept. This was Dan after he had shown up in Jessie's room with a murder kit and faithfully and ruthlessly executed his plan. This was Dan just minutes after he left our house.

We watched the video.

"Hi, Dan. Thanks for coming in. You are not in any trouble. You are not under arrest. You can leave at any time. We just want to ask you some questions in the hopes that you can give us some information that might help us solve this case. Would you answer a few questions? Do you want something to drink?"

The officer from the Washington County Sheriff's Department had done well. He established immediately that Dan was there voluntarily, a key point under Miranda Law. He left the door to the interview room open, so no claim could be made later that the defendant might have felt intimidated or detained despite being told that he was free to go at any time. He was offered something to drink and bathroom breaks so that it could not be argued later that comforts were denied. He was in no way tricky or deceitful, but he played on a liar's instinct to pretend to help.

He did not read Dan his Miranda rights. He didn't have to. Dan was there voluntarily and not under arrest.

"Thanks for coming in so fast when I called you, Dan. How did you get here?"

"Jackie and Amelia drove me in."

"And where were you when I called you?"

"I was at the Blodgett house."

You could have heard a pin drop in the courtroom as the video drama unfolded. You could see in the interviewing officer's face the light bulb go on. You could see his mind racing.

At the time, they had called Dan in to ask him about the attack on Melissa Richards in Richfield. Remember, in an astonishing and heroic display of clarity under pressure, Melissa not only fought her attacker off, but also had the presence of mind to describe him and his van to police. They had connected him to the van in the park, but they had not connected him to Jessie's death yet.

Now, he was connecting himself.

The officer went on. "The Blodgett house...isn't that the girl in Hartford?"

"Yeah," Dan replied.

"Yeah, what happened to her?"

"She was raped and murdered."

It was a moment I will never forget. Back on July 16, 2013, the day of this interview, nobody, not even the police, knew that Jess had been sexually assaulted before she was strangled to death.

Well, nobody except Dan.

At that time, Chief Groves told us that the initial physical exam showed no signs of sexual assault. It was not until weeks later, when reports came back from the State Crime Lab that we learned semen was found, with DNA, and that Jess had been raped. That DNA analysis would implicate the accused. But here he was on video, implicating himself the day after he did it.

We would hear later in the hearing from District Attorney Bensen that the accused, when confronted with his lie about the job he never had, eventually admitted to being in the park and having an altercation with Melissa Richards. He claimed he was just trying to scare her and never intended any harm. But when he was asked to put his story in writing, he decided that he needed an attorney.

The video showed how, as soon as Dan asked for an attorney, the interview stopped. As frustrating as it must have been for detectives to be so close to a confession, they knew that by law they could not proceed without an attorney present. They left the room. They were now forced to make a quick and critical decision. Arrest Dan and charge him, or let him go.

The officers re-entered the room, put Dan under arrest, and read him his Miranda rights. They could ask him no more questions about the event in the park without an attorney present.

I was impressed with how professionally the police handled this first interview. They got a lot of damning information. And, under pressure, they had stayed within all boundaries of the law and the suspect's rights. At least it looked that way to me.

Then came the second interview the following day on July 17, 2013. The Washington County Sheriff's Office had contacted the Hartford P.D. They explained what went down in that first interview and told them they appeared to have a person of interest in the Jessie Blodgett homicide.

Detective Thickens interviewed the suspect.

We watched the video as Thickens asked if Dan would be willing to answer some questions and help the police gather information regarding Jessie's case. Dan agreed.

The video ended.

It was now Defense Attorney Schmaus's turn. He argued convincingly the suspect should never have been questioned without an attorney present on the seventeenth after asking for an attorney on the sixteenth.

The State argued, with equal effectiveness, that the interview on the seventeenth was about a different crime and different charges than the one that Dan had requested legal counsel for. The State further argued that Dan had been read his Miranda rights on the sixteenth, and that he voluntarily consented to Detective Thickens' request for an interview, fully aware that he didn't have to talk.

It was in the judge's hands.

With astute reasoning and clarity, Judge Martins explained every noteworthy point from both the Prosecution and the Defense's viewpoints. He again cited precedent cases in Wisconsin law.

My heart rate rose and fell with every sway back and forth in his methodical analysis. It felt like the fourth quarter of a tight Super Bowl game with emotions at fever pitch, only much worse. This was no game. This was real life. The whole case was at stake here.

Joy clutched my hand tighter. We could sense the judge winding down his review. The ruling was coming. Up to this point in the legal process, since the first hearing over eight months ago, it seemed to us that the defendant had all the rights, all the protections. If he was protected again, and key evidence suppressed, I didn't know what I would do. If our system let us down, let Jess down, and let Dan walk, I wasn't sure if I could take it.

And then the ruling came.

"Motion to suppress denied."

chapter forty-one

THE TREE

"Mama help me fathom
All these people feeling so random.
I just can't relate."
—Jessie Blodgett, "Overnight"

FOUR SIMPLE WORDS: MOTION TO suppress denied. The world felt different as we rose from the classic oak benches this time, like the sun was trying to peek out from behind thick cloud cover that had obscured it for a long time.

Joy and I weren't looking to this trial for vengeance and retribution, and we weren't looking for closure either. We knew closure was a myth. Closure was something talked about by people whose only child wasn't gone forever. But rather, we were hoping the Truth would come out. We didn't hate Dan. We had forgiven him every day for nine months now.

Don't get me wrong. We needed him held accountable for his actions. It would have been a second injustice if that didn't happen.

Everyone should be accountable for their actions, including me. And, of course, we knew how sick and dangerous he was, and that he could never be allowed the freedom to harm anyone again.

But it was the truth that we needed most. We wanted an end to rumors, gossip and speculation. We wanted an end to the silence that we were advised to keep. We wanted the whole world to know exactly what had and had not happened that Monday morning in mid-July in Jessie's bedroom.

We wanted the whole world to know this wasn't an "accident" that she had participated in, a bondage game gone wrong. We wanted the gossipers to see how wrong they were and hopefully feel some remorse for their hurtful and unfounded speculations. In a small town church in Canada, a family friend asked Joy's mom, "What did she do to make him so mad?" As if Jessie had done something that caused Dan to do this. What kind of a question is that, and how could you ask it of her grandma?

It finally looked like we were getting a little closer to the day the whole truth would come out.

On our way out, we passed Skip and Laura and their large family again. They both hugged Joy and me, and we exchanged brief blessings and sympathies. Then two of Skip's sisters came to me and said, "Thank you for the grace you have shown our family."

That meant everything. The fact that two families on opposite sides of a murder trial could show each other respect, empathy, and love meant everything. It brought hope for the world back into my heart. It brought faith in the goodness of people, and a small measure of healing back into our families. I will always appreciate them for that.

The unusually long and cold Wisconsin winter finally yielded to spring. The snow melted, the daffodils and tulips popped up through the thawing ground, and the cold April rains reluctantly gave way to May sunshine and green grass. Our spirits seemed to rise with the lengthening days and the rising temperatures.

It was finally time to plant the tree—a butterfly magnolia. Being marginal in our zone, the planting of Jessie's butterfly magnolia had to wait until spring.

As you might suspect, there is a story here.

In September of 2013, seven months before Judge Martens would deny the Defense's motion to suppress evidence and two months after Jess left us, we got a call from the Hartford Parks and Recreation Department.

I returned the call and asked for Mike, the guy who had left the message.

"Hi Mike, it's Buck Blodgett."

"Oh, hi, Buck. Hey, I had called to tell you someone paid for a tree in memory of your daughter. I wanted to talk with you about what kind of a tree you want, and where you want it planted."

"Wow. Who did that?"

"Someone named Barbie. She donated two hundred and fifty dollars toward a tree of your choosing. You can have it planted in any city park in Hartford. We'll do it for you. We just need to know what tree you want, and where you want it."

Barbie Orban. Barbie who sent me *Jesus Calling* in February; Barbie, my childhood friend from across the street, the girl who ran away at age twelve and now shared her survival story through Celebrate Recovery and Exploit No More.

Barbie's family had a tree, too, in memory of her older brother, John.

Mike said, "Why don't you and Joy think it over and call me back."

"Will do, Mike. Thanks a lot."

"But, hey, I just gotta tell you I've been doing a little research about butterfly trees. I've heard about your butterfly stories, and I wondered if you might want one. I've got some species and pricing info if you're interested. Just let me know; I can forward it to you."

"I like that idea, Mike. Thanks. Sure, please forward the info. Joy and I will look it over."

I hung up with Mike and called Barbie.

"Barbie, thank you so much. What a beautiful gift. You should not have spent two hundred and fifty dollars."

"I didn't. I rounded up three friends to pitch in with me."

"Wow, really...? People have been so amazing. Very cool of three strangers to pitch in that much. I want to thank them. Can you get me their contact info?"

"They're not strangers. They all know you. You remember Lori Napholz from the old neighborhood, right?

"Yeah, sure." Wow, that was forty years ago. Nice to hear that Barbie and Lori were still friends. I also knew Lori from my brother Dana's tavern in Milwaukee.

"And Margo Lucas. She used to see you in your old clinic in the Falls."

"What? Margo? I haven't seen her since I left the Falls twelve years ago. Her whole family used to come in. They were some of my very favorite patients. How did she happen to pitch in with you?"

"We're good friends. And Tracy Shimetz too."

"What? Tracy and her boys are some of my favorite patients now in the West Allis clinic. How did she find out about your tree donation?"

"We're best friends too."

"No way."

There are over two million people in Greater Milwaukee and beyond. I was amazed everybody knew everybody. I was trying to piece it together. "Wait, I get it," I said. "You all went to St. Bernard's together, then moved around when you grew up. That's funny, I never knew Margo and Tracy grew up in Tosa."

"They didn't," Barbie said. "We became friends after school, when we were older."

The world suddenly seemed a little smaller.

And the connections grew.

This would happen again to me later in the year. The design of the world and the people in it was shifting. I was starting to see the Great Weaver's web.

The following week, I called Mike back at the Rec Center.

"Hey, Mike. Joy and I have been thinking. We like your idea of a butterfly tree. We haven't figured out which one though."

"Good, because I found another one that I think is really cool. It's a butterfly magnolia. I'll look into it more if you like it. We're in a marginal zone, but I already talked with Black's Nursery, and they said it will be fine here."

"Mike, do you know where Jessie was born?"

"No, why?"

"She was born in Georgia, where Joy and I went to chiropractic school. I'm not sure, but I think maybe the magnolia is the state tree of Georgia. They're all over down there. They're beautiful. Great big

188

flowering blossoms all spring. Joy loved them. They were our favorite tree."

"Wow, that's funny. I'll check into them further and see if we can get you one."

"Sounds good, thanks."

"Which park do you want it planted in?" Mike asked.

"Well, Jess and I spent a lot of time at Pike Lake State Park, by our house. But that's not a city park, so that's probably out, right?"

"Yeah, I mean we could give you the tree to plant there, but if you put it in a city park, we would take care of it for you."

"There's no park in the city that was really meaningful to Jess. But, you know, she took swimming lessons, basketball, tennis, and ballet at the Rec Center when she was little. And she performed in high school plays, musicals, and concerts at the Schauer Arts Center right next door. I don't want to ask too much, but is it possible to plant the tree on Rec Center property between the two buildings?"

"There's an easement between the two properties. Let me check into that, and see what we can do."

And so it was done. The butterfly magnolia would be planted on the easement near the front entrance to the Schauer Arts Center, where Jess had so many life moments, and where she played the Fiddler in The Hartford Players' *Fiddler on the Roof* on each of the last three days of her life.

Hundreds of people would file in and out of the Arts Center every few weeks, passing her tree, passing the plaque beneath it.

Jessie Blodgett
1994 ~ 2013
"Fly Free"
LOVE > hate

They would see it and remember her. Many of them had seen Jess perform. Some had performed with her. They would sigh, smile, and maybe talk about her for a minute. Hearts would beat a little harder and heads would shake, in memory of Jess.

And they would be reminded of the legacy she has left this world.

ⓕ Buck Blodgett

May 10, 2014

Butterfly magnolia planted today for you, Jess. Next week it will bloom and the butterflies will come. Thirty family and friends spread the dirt, mulch, and memories. You were there too. Thank you, Barb Orban, Lori Napholz O'Connell, Margo and Jim Lucas, and Tracy Schimetz for the tree. Thank you, Dillon Connor, for the plaque. Thank you Mike & Beth Hermann for all the arrangements.

Now, when people visit the Schauer Arts Center for shows, they will remember you, and they will know that LOVE>hate. You touched many, sweetie, and you remain forever in our hearts.

I said a few words at the tree planting.

"If we were all souls, waiting in Heaven, ready to be placed into a body and into a life…. If we were in line, and our turn was coming…. If we could choose our parents, our family, and the life lessons ahead…and if the Angel said, 'This one will end badly. You will only live for nineteen years, and you will die violently, but…you will make a bigger difference in your nineteen years than most do in a lifetime. You will touch many, and you will begin a legacy that will bring more Love and Forgiveness into the world....'

"I'm not saying this is literally true, but if.... Jess would have been at the front of the line."

I have no idea where that came from. I probably stole it from someone that I can't credit now. But Pastor John brought it up time and again, as if Jessie actually did that.

Isn't my pastor cool?

chapter forty-two

MOTION TO CHANGE VENUE

"Help me understand it
And just maybe I can mend it,
And teach you how to live again."
—Jessie Blodgett, "Overnight"

THERE WERE SMILES AND TEARS at the tree planting, but more smiles. Except for Joy. She was just terribly sad. It wasn't so much the event, but what was coming next. The day after was Mother's Day.

Everyone sensed that Mother's Day would be hard for Joy, like Christmas was, like Thanksgiving, and like Jessie's birthday.

But for Joy, Mother's Day was the worst of all. No one who has not lost a child, especially an only child, could possibly understand what this day meant to her. Even I couldn't understand, until she told me.

Joy thought she'd be a mother for the rest of her life. It never occurred to her that she could be ejected from the mother's club. The one day of the year for her to be appreciated for a lifetime of sacrifice and unconditional love, and here she was suddenly childless at the age of fifty-four. She wasn't in the mother's club anymore.

When you become a mom, "Mom" becomes the central core of your identity. It's who you are. It's what you do. It's your role in life. You stake your place in the structure of those closest to you, those you love most, with that identity. And when you're a mom whose only child is suddenly stolen, the core of your identity is stolen too. Who you are is gone. There's nothing much left. Joy was nothing now.

You can't go back to being a carefree teenager. You're too old for that. You had a purpose, and someone who would always need you. Suddenly, you didn't.

Never again will you go out with your girlfriends and feel like you belong. They will all talk about their kids, not to be insensitive or mean, but because their kids are the central core of their identities. Their kids are who they are. They don't know what else to talk about.

You don't want to be the death of the party, so you nod, and smile, and listen to the stories about their kids, and then you excuse yourself a little early when you can't stand the pain anymore. Your girlfriends all feel bad that you left, and so do you. Now it's awkward. Now it will be worse next time.

It's no one's fault.

They couldn't keep from talking about their kids any more than the sun could keep from coming up.

And you couldn't have tried any harder to be okay with it.

But it's not okay. It will never be okay. Nothing will ever be okay again. Your identity was stolen. It's gone forever, and nothing—no friends, no LOVE>hate Project, no amount of years, will ever change that fact. Period.

For Joy, the number of days in the calendar year should be three hundred and sixty-four, and Mother's Day should be left out.

On May 29, Joy and I were back at the Washington County Courthouse in West Bend. My family was waiting again on the concrete walkway. We made our way through the glass entranceway to the courthouse, said hello to the security officers as we passed through the metal detectors, and continued on through the hallway outside the courtrooms.

Joy and I had both commented on the drive up that we'd like to reach out to Skip and Laura again, and maybe talk just a bit more this time. I wondered if they had the same idea when I spotted their whole family gathered just past security. Normally, their group was further down the hall, by the courtroom entrance.

Joy and I came through the door and spilled right into their circle. We felt their eyes and energy shift to us.

I feel like our culture dictates that there's supposed to be tension and hostility when things like this happen. But we didn't feel that. We felt their deep sorrow and regret. We also felt welcomed.

Joy and I made our way around their family circle, one person at a time. It just took a minute or two, but we hugged each one, and exchanged a few words and tears.

Not all of the minutes in a person's life are equal. Those two minutes of my life were not equal to the two before them, or the two after. Those two minutes were rare. They were sent to me, to all of us, from the Higher Place.

I know Dan's family was in great pain. I hope they don't think I'm insensitive or nuts, but if a chasm as big as this one could be bridged so easily—in minutes—then the future of humanity may not be so dark after all, and peace might be closer than we think.

We left Skip, Laura and their group and moved down the hallway to wait with my family until the courtroom opened. Two of Dan's aunts followed.

They approached Joy. "What can our family do to honor Jessie?" one of them asked.

"Well…there's a memorial fund in her name," Joy said after she thanked them. "The proceeds go either to the Jessie Blodgett Music Scholarship Program at Central Middle School, where she loved to give lessons to the kids in orchestra, or to The LOVE>hate Project to raise awareness about male on female violence."

I should have kept quiet, but I couldn't help myself. I thought it would be an amazing opportunity for healing, an amazing example for our culture: if two families on opposite sides of a murder trial could join together in love and forgiveness and unite to share a powerful message. And so I said that.

I have not heard from them since. I can understand why. Life has dealt them all a horribly painful blow, through no fault of their own. It's not fair. I want all of Dan's family to know I have empathy and admiration for them, and I want them to know my invitation to join and work together will always be open.

The doors opened and we all went to our usual seats, friends of the bride on the left, friends of the groom on the right. District Attorney Bensen, Assistant D.A. Giernoth, and Victim/Witness Coordinator Ali, entered. As always, they came to Joy and me and said hi.

Maybe it was more like a recurring funeral than a wedding. People just kept coming up to us and paying their respects. Ali invited us up to the D.A.'s office after court to talk about the case, as she always did.

The door at the back of the courtroom opened. In came Dan, in orange jumpsuit and shackles, escorted by the same two deputies. I searched his face and his eyes. I don't know what I was looking for, something, anything, maybe some sign that he now understood the magnitude of what he had done, some sign of honesty, or regret.

His eyes briefly panned his side of the courtroom, but not ours. They never came to our side anymore, not since the first hearing. His grin was gone today. He looked different to me, tired, concerned maybe. I imagined that things had changed for him after the last court date, since the evidence was all ruled admissible. I imagined that the fantasy he was living was starting to crack and crumble.

"All rise."

Judge Martens entered.

"Thank you. Be seated." The judge continued, "We are here today to consider the Defense's motion to change venue. The basic issue is this: has media coverage and public conversation been such that we would not be able to select a jury pool from Washington County that would be unbiased and not prejudicial against the defendant? We must ensure that the defendant has a fair trial. His case must be heard by an unbiased and objective jury of his peers.

"Before we begin with the motion to change venue, Mr. Schmaus, I understand that the Defense wishes to withdraw one of its two pleas, the 'not guilty by reason of mental defect' plea? Is that correct?"

"Yes it is, Your Honor."

The judge asked the Defense Attorney and the defendant a series of questions to ensure that this was properly addressed, and to establish that this was Dan's wish, and he understood and owned his choice.

Joy and I looked at each other, surprised. He's withdrawing not guilty by reason of mental defect? Apparently the Defense's second opinion, from their own doctor, was not favorable for Dan.

Was this good or bad? Did this raise the likelihood he would employ the only defense we imagined he could try? Did this mean the Defense would claim this was a case of consensual sex gone wrong? —A terrible accident followed by panic and a lie, but not murder? What else could they try, if he was not insane? He couldn't just stick to his old story: "I wasn't there, and I didn't do it." Mountains of DNA said otherwise.

We feared the dishonest smearing of Jessie's reputation and name. It was so unfair. She could not defend herself. She could not face this liar and call him on his BS. Her voice was stolen with her life.

To Dan's credit, he never claimed this. But that didn't stop Joy from worrying about it for thirteen months, because Dan also never admitted he did it. He never confessed, pled guilty, and ended this monthly parade to the courthouse that caused so many people so much pain.

Judge Martens then began addressing the motion to change venue. He did his usual brilliant review. He covered every example of media exposure the Defense had submitted to him—the TV stories, newspapers articles, radio spots, and even social media conversations.

But his review and explanation was different this time. In the past, it seemed that he took roughly equal time stating the cases of both parties. This time, it was a landslide for the Prosecution. Every item, right down the line, was a clear point in the State's favor, it seemed. If it would have been a football game, the score would have been forty to zero.

"Motion to change venue denied."

We didn't really even care so much about this motion. If we had to travel to a different county, so what? Or if they brought in jurors from outside of Washington County, so what? After the Defense's motion to suppress evidence was denied the prior month, everything had changed for us. Nothing else mattered. Now we knew all the facts would come out. The truth would come out. Where it happened or in front of what jury seemed secondary.

Still, it was another win for Jessie and for justice. It was the second win in a row, after nine months of frustration, nine months of waiting, and nine months of worrying that a jury might not be allowed to know the whole truth. And the surprise bonus today was that the Defense had taken the 'not guilty by reason of mental defect' plea off the table.

The tide had turned.

chapter forty-three

MILKWEED

"So if you try and fail
The sun won't set.
Just don't give up,
You're not done yet."

— Jessie Blodgett, "Overnight"

THE PRECURSOR TO THIS BOOK was the butterfly stories. In fact, it was always after reading the butterfly stories that people would say to me: "You have to write a book." At first I brushed them off. I didn't have time to write a book. But eventually I saw the light.

The butterfly stories began in the hotel room the night after Jessie's death when I asked God to show me if He was really here. I was talking to myself, honestly. I didn't expect an answer. What followed was a series of unusual butterfly events accompanied by the deep Peace. To anyone on the outside, these events would seem like stories, but to the involved parties they were moments of truth.

After several months, when they kept occurring, I began taking notes. There was something crazy going on, and I didn't want to let the details dissolve into foggy memories.

In Jessie's first message, delivered to me by Laura Gruber on January 31, 2014, she said: **Butterflies everywhere, Dad. I'll share them with you.** Since then, I've been buried in butterflies.

There were butterfly calendars, ceramic butterflies, sketched butterflies. We were given butterfly nightlights, butterfly ID books, and a common milkweed plant with a tag explaining milkweed is being lost to development, and it's the only plant that monarchs lay their eggs on. (There is a movement to save the monarch by reestablishing milkweed.)

There was a butterfly glass sculpture, a butterfly image embedded in glass, and a butterfly ashtray in our growing collection. Three different patients brought me stick-on butterflies with flashing lights. They adorn the windows in my two treatment rooms at the clinic. A friend took an old attic window and turned into art with two big butterflies on it. There were a dozen butterfly stories in an article from Compassionate Friends, a support group for those who've lost loved ones. There were multiple decorative garden plaques with…wait for it…butterflies on them. There was a butterfly wall hanging and two butterfly Christmas tree ornaments. On and on it went.

The word was obviously out. I could no longer consider the timely appearance of a butterfly a sign. I stopped taking notes, and the butterfly stories ended at twelve, the last one being the chimes at 5:40 a.m. on New Year's Day.

Four days after Judge Martens denied the change of venue motion, and two weeks after we planted the tree, I returned to the Rec Center with a "thank you" card for Mike.

Mike wasn't in. I left the card. Afterward, I stopped outside to visit the tree. I sat down on the bench, in the shade of Jessie's tree, and prayed a little. I talked quietly to my beautiful girl, and asked God to make sure she was happy.

As I rose to go, looking over my shoulder to say goodbye, I looked down to the ground. Behind the bench, milkweed shoots were popping up through the mulch.

I looked around. The garden was immaculately landscaped, and there were almost no other weeds in it, except a little grass around the edges. I strolled around the grounds to survey all the gardens in front of the Schauer Arts Center and Rec Center. There were no weeds, and no sign of any other milkweed in the whole complex.

But here it was. It had not come in with the root ball of the magnolia tree. It was several feet off to the side. No, it had come in with the wind, by chance. Chance apparently thought Jessie's butterfly magnolia would be the perfect spot for a new natural colony of common milkweed.

P.S. There were exactly twenty new milkweed shoots coming up. Okay, maybe I'm reaching now, but remember who just had her 20th birthday in March....

Buck Blodgett
June 15, 2014

Eleven months, right about now, and counting, Jess. Tired of the pain. Getting used to it. Thankful for the joy. I see you everywhere, climbing in the apple trees, in your room at bedtime, in the little girl on TV last night with the olives on her fingertips. I hear your voice singing in my head as I drive, whispering encouragement and direction when I'm lost.

Sweetie, I've been learning from you.

We are all in this together, and we must all get out of this together, every last one of us. Everyone counts, everyone matters. No one can be left out. LOVE THEM ALL.

We have a lot of work to do. (74 school shootings since Sandy Hook.)

This is school, and we are all sleeping in class. Our bodies are rentals. Every second and every choice counts.

Pain is a gift that deepens our capacity to Love, just as freezing rain deepens our appreciation of a warm house.

Love you forever, angel.

Your time is coming. Your voice will be heard....

chapter forty-four

THE PRESENTERS

"Close your eyes,
You've just begun."
—Jessie Blodgett, "Overnight"

LATE JUNE, A WEEK AFTER this post, I found myself at, where else, the Perc Place. We were about to have our first official meeting for The LOVE>hate Project. I was excited. It was a gathering of the presenters, and I couldn't wait for them to get to know each other.

The presenters would be our future speakers, the people who would take our message public when the trial was over. There were five people, plus me, who had a strong affinity for our cause. They were people who had placed themselves into my life, listened, and been there for me through the pain—just plain beautiful humans with giant hearts. I loved every one of them.

John was the first person this atheist ever called his pastor, the East Coaster whose kind eyes belied his intimidating size when he bellowed to visitors they weren't welcome to coffee until their third service. John watched my video and told me to get ready. John listened to me without judgment. John interviewed me in front of his church and likened me to Mother Teresa. (I turned red. As you all know, I am no Mother Teresa, but then, she probably wasn't either.) He expanded my understanding of what was happening here.

Pastor John didn't think he should be a presenter. "Everyone else has a powerful personal story or expertise to share. I'm just a preacher."

But I had heard him speak. I had *felt* him speak. When John talks, people expand, and Love and Forgiveness materialize in a manly way. We needed a man like that.

Barbie. Her survival story as a young girl on the streets of Milwaukee speaks for itself. She was already involved in fighting human trafficking. She gave us the tree. She gave me *Jesus Calling*.

Laura. Not only did she get messages from dead people, she also taught anti-bullying classes in Hartford, and had her own powerful personal story. Much like mine, hers involved her daughter. Laura had given me *Awaken the Spirit Within*.

Nancy. She's the mom of two of Jessie's high school friends, and the youngest of eighteen siblings. Those eighteen siblings shared five different parents. There was verbal, physical, and sexual abuse. If anyone has a survival story to match Barbie's, it's Nancy.

Nancy will not tell you this, but she's a talented writer. Of the one thousand-plus letters and cards we received after Jessie's funeral, Nancy wrote my all-time favorite. She captured the essence of Jess in words like no one ever has.

One day, she emailed me a story she wrote, *Fuschia's Garden*. It was an allegory of Jessie's life and death—a children's story about a beautiful flower in a garden that was harmed by the jealous garden tool who tended her. Nancy's story is far more digestible for elementary school kids than mine. It was the perfect answer to the question: How do we share our disturbing but important messages with children?

And finally, Kelly. Kelly and her family have been patients of mine for over a dozen years. I've watched her kids grow up.

One day a couple years ago, it dawned on me that I didn't even know what she did. She never talked about herself. She was always interested in serving others, including me, even though it was supposed to be the other way around. I got over my embarrassment and finally asked.

Kelly is a trauma counselor. A jobsite for her usually involves death and shock. Her clients range from everyday people to celebrities. She is the expert's expert at bringing Love into situations of loss and tragedy.

Kelly also didn't know if she would "fit" on our Presenters Team. She knew violence and loss and Love. She had plenty of personal stories from her job, but she couldn't share them; they were confidential.

The Presenters met several times, and our plans crystallized. Barbie, Nancy, and I would tell our stories of physical and sexual violence to teens and adults. Laura would take our message to elementary and middle schools. She would follow Nancy's children's story (performed as a short drama), with her own teachings about bullying and Love.

John would be our MC. If anyone could lend credibility and create interest just by introducing a person, it was John.

And Kelly would be our expert. It was Kelly who clued me in that many people would be triggered by our messages, and that we needed to be ready to support those people with trained professionals.

We had accidentally put together a complete and perfect team. Well, maybe not accidentally. Yes, I keep saying things like that. That's because they keep happening.

I love the Presenters. We had a cause we believed in and felt compelled to share. Even those who thought they didn't fit.

A week later, on June 29, I was walking around "the Zone." The Zone (short for construction zone) is what Jess and I called the new development at the end of old Wayside Drive. It used to be a farmers' field, full of turkeys, deer, rabbits, and the occasional snake. When we moved here in May of 1999, Wayside Drive was a dead end cul-de-sac that ended at the field. We liked it that way.

We were against the new development. But when construction started, Jess and I looked at the positives. We would have new neighbors, an infusion of kids in our aging neighborhood for Jess to make friends with, and a three-quarter-mile loop we could walk around.

I ran Milo around the Zone twice a day for most of his life. Jess often joined us. I used to know half the families in the Zone, like the Dobners, because of my dog and my daughter. I knew the neighbors with dogs the best, because our dogs always stopped to greet each other, so we had to greet each other too. We should all try to be a little more like dogs.

I rarely go around the Zone nowadays. It's not the same anymore without Jess and Milo.

But after dark that evening, I decided to go again. As I walked around alone, I kind of prayed. *Jesus Calling* had been training me to remember the presence of God throughout my day, talk to Him, and thank Him. Gratitude was key to receiving His blessings. That would have sounded like somebody's religious BS to me last year. Now it sounded like a discipline I wanted to develop.

So what the hell, I prayed. If I wasn't thinking about something worthwhile, I would slip into sadness anyway. I started thanking God for whatever came to mind.

One thing was my guardian angel, which came to mind because of *Awaken the Spirit Within*. I never believed in them. I still don't know if I do, but I want to (because of what happened next).

I reached the top of the hill, right by Scott and Greta's house. They were the first new friends we ever made in the Zone. They had a dog and kids, so naturally we became friends. Milo used to stop and say hi to their dog, and Jess used to babysit for them. Now, Milo is gone, their dog is gone, and Jess is gone. I guess Scott, Greta, and I will be gone too, one day.

Anyway, as I was walking along in the dark, thanking God for my guardian angel, which I didn't really believe in, it occurred to me to ask: "Jess, are you my guardian angel?" The moment I finished asking, the streetlight above me went out.

Awaken the Spirit Within says there are some common signs of the presence of our departed loved ones. Sometimes they are electrical, like lights flickering on and off. I had just read that part.

When I finished my walk I told Joy what happened. Looking back, I'm surprised I told her. She wasn't overly fond of my butterfly stories or my newfound faith.

Maybe too many people had said things to her like, "It's God's plan." They meant well, but nothing bothered her more.

"God planned for Jessie to be raped and strangled?" she'd ask me privately. She wasn't really mad at God, just heartbroken and tired of people trying to cheer her up with their religion. What good were their beliefs to her? Did they bring Jessie back, or help them understand her anguish and be better listeners? Usually not. Their beliefs often crowded out their empathy.

Anyway, I told Joy about the streetlight. Instead of a cynical comment, she shared a memory.

On July 16, 2013, the day after Jess was murdered, Joy walked into our upstairs bathroom. No one was over yet. Soon all the kids would come, including Dan, and the vigil would begin. While Joy was standing in the bathroom, one of the light bulbs at the top of the mirror exploded. Yes, it spontaneously burst into hundreds of little pieces. Not when she turned the light on; it was already on. It exploded as she stood there.

I don't know; I'm not a fix-it guy. Do light bulbs do that sometimes? Maybe you've seen light bulbs spontaneously explode before, the day after someone is murdered and the murderer is about to knock on your door.

A MESSAGE TO JESSIE

To the lovely girl who didn't leave thoughts and words unsaid or life untasted.... To the only nineteen-year-old conscientious enough to write a letter to humanity.... To the ever thoughtful one, whose deep brown eyes seemed to discern the wisdom of the world, yet still twinkled with joy and laughter: You charmed us, you challenged us; you dazzled and inspired us. So confident and free to be yourself.... So encouraging of others to do the same.... The world is a better place because you were in it.... Yours is a sacred story, Jessie. You had open eyes. You noticed. You listened. You shared the song of your heart. Some grow old and draw near death only to discover that they never really lived! Not so with you.... A voice as lovely as yours cannot be silenced: It will live in our hearts, in our memories, and in those who you've inspired to sing.

A light as bright as yours could never be put out.

—Nancy Baumhardt

chapter forty-five

THE ANNIVERSARY

"Love your life,
You just got one."
—Jessie Blodgett, "Overnight"

JULY OF 2014 STARTED OUT busy. That was good; being busy helped. We didn't want to sit around and think about the impending one-year anniversary of Jessie's passing.

The Fourth of July reunion with my long-lost cousins in Ohio; the Color Run; the Consultants Academy; the next status hearing at the courthouse; and the formation of our new Board of Directors for The LOVE>hate Project were all coming in July. It would be a little crazy, but it was good.

On July third, Joy and I piled into the van with my mom and Becky for the road trip to Ohio. They weren't exactly lost, these cousins of mine. Mom and Becky had seen them many times over the years. It was me who had been lost. I'd hardly seen them since I was a kid, mostly because I was too busy trying to get ahead.

Those days are over, thank God. Like I said earlier, I don't care about most of the stuff I used to care about. I just want to connect with quality people. And cousins Sue, Scott, Deb, Jeff, and Aunt Polly are quality people, every one.

They were Uncle Bud's kids. Uncle Bud, my mom's brother, died in June. When we decided to go to our cousin's family reunion, I was so looking forward to seeing Uncle Bud again. But I didn't get my priorities straight in time, and so we added a funeral to our itinerary.

It's funny how funerals make us appreciate life and each other. Having had two funerals in twelve months, I was more grateful for life and the people in it. I wish all humans had an appreciation for life and each other regardless of whether a funeral was happening.

How many days in a row can a person cry? Well, at least three hundred and fifty-four. I know that because, as of our Fourth of July trip to Ohio, Joy cried every day since she lost Jess.

Some may think it's time for her to move on, but not those who have lost a child, especially an only child. Those who have lost the core of their identity understand how it feels when there's nothing left.

I don't feel like Joy is nothing. She does. I feel like she is still a wife whose husband loves her. I feel like she is still a doctor whose patients love her. She knows that. She wants to feel like those things too. She can't help how she feels. She just feels like a mom who doesn't have her only daughter anymore.

Despite Joy's tears, the four of us had a surprisingly fun road trip. Cousin Rick drove out solo and joined us. My brother, Fred, came from Maine. Fred and I were at least talking again. We didn't have much to say, but we were at least talking. Why is it so hard for people to work through conflict, even two good people who love each other?

We had a great time catching up with the clan. The fireworks were the most spectacular I've ever seen, including the ones at Summerfest on the Lakefront in Milwaukee. My cousins were famous for their annual fireworks extravaganza, and they did not disappoint. We all sat on the deck overlooking the pond in the backyard, explosions all around.

I asked Cousin Sue, "How in the world do you ever get away with this without your neighbors calling the police?"

"They're all here!" she laughed while offering Joy another glass of wine.

It was truly an unforgettable show, an hour straight of what would have been the grand finale for most fireworks displays. From the bottle rocket lighting of the Mega Bonfire, to the five sticks of real dynamite lobbed over the pond that sent shockwaves right through us to close the night, it was a sight to behold.

But the highlight of the weekend for me was unexpected. I showed The LOVE>hate Project's three-minute trailer. I didn't really plan to, and I thought maybe I shouldn't because it was their family reunion and they were mourning Uncle Bud. This wasn't about Joy and me, and Jessie. But I was a little out of control by that point, paying less attention than ever to social norms, hungering to talk with people about violence and Love and our cause.

As it turned out, the small group that first watched it in Sue's bedroom, where all the family dogs were jailed for the evening, was moved. So they asked if I would play it again, and they left to rally more viewers. And then those people told more, and so on, until I had shown the video five or six times to dozens of people.

Even people who didn't know me before that night, who never knew Jessie, from several states away, who were in no way connected with our community were touched by this video. My belief in what we were trying to do went to the next level in Ohio.

Now my long-lost cousins support The LOVE>hate Project on Facebook. I see their "likes" and their comments and I remember old times playing together as kids. I regret how competitive I was, and how long it took me to get my priorities straight. But it's never too late to love people again.

Mom, Becky, Joy, and I piled in the van on Saturday, the day after the Fourth of July, and road-tripped it back to Wisconsin. We had to get back. The Color Run was coming on Sunday.

We were in it because of Laura and Emily Gruber, or maybe because of Jessie. In one of the messages, Laura said Jess told her that I was wondering about colors: **Yes, gold and grey—trust, yes, it is me. He wants to know colors. Pink, blue, rainbow stuff too. COLORS!** (We chose our original website and PowerPoint colors from this message.)

In an unrelated matter (if there is such a thing), Laura and Emily were searching for the Illumination Run online to find information and register, but found the Color Run by accident.

So on July sixth, nine days before the first anniversary of Jessie's passing, I found myself on a bus with eighty runners and volunteers. We left Hartford Union High School at 5:00 a.m. for Miller Park in Milwaukee. Laura and Emily had built Team Butterfly Kisses for Jessie.

Half of us were running the race. The rest were volunteers, waiting at stations to color bomb the runners with bright powder packets.

213

I had blue under my toenails for about two weeks. Jess would have been so down for this event. What a blast we all had in her memory. The volunteer color bombers were almost unrecognizable. They must have gotten bored between runners and gone after each other.

Laura and Emily recruited forty volunteers. The Color Run paid us forty dollars per volunteer, so the event raised sixteen hundred dollars for The LOVE>hate Project. They had team T-shirts designed, booked the bus, picked up registration packets, and did countless other things.

Barbie Orban leaned on a couple friends and arranged for a post-event police motorcycle escort from Miller Park to the local bar/restaurant she managed, where she sprang for pizza and soda.

People just kept giving, supporting our mission, and honoring Jess, even if it meant having blue toenails for weeks.

Three days after that, on July 9 and 10, I attended a two-day educational seminar: the Consultant's Academy.

A couple months prior, I was at Jimmy II's in Slinger, having breakfast with Pastor John and Pat Quinn. John said I needed to meet Pat. I wasn't clear exactly why, but with the way things had been going since July of 2013, I figured he was right.

Pat attended our church in Cedar Springs. He was a teacher-turned-educational consultant. Basically, he taught teachers how to quit their day jobs by becoming consultants like him. Educational consultants teach the teachers. Pat's the guy who teaches the teachers' teachers.

Pat is the nation's leading expert in RTI (Response to Intervention), a tiered approach to assisting kids with learning disabilities. After watching our video, he invited me to attend his four-hundred-

and-fifty-dollar seminar for free. Pat knew the power of a good
course, because he once attended one when he was on the verge of
quitting teaching, and it changed his life forever.

One of the many things I got out of it was that even though I
was a round peg in a square hole (the only attendee who wasn't an
educator), dozens of teachers who didn't know me and would never
see me again all agreed this message needed to be heard in schools.

I learned another important thing in Pat's seminar: I should write
this book. A few people had suggested that already, but I dismissed
it. I didn't want to write a book, and I didn't have time. I didn't even
have time to start a new nonprofit organization. I certainly didn't
want to add another boulder to the load.

But Pat said to effectively speak in schools around the country
you need to write a book. That changed my thinking. I guess that's
what consultants do—they change the way you think.

I hope this book changes *your* thinking. I feel like my Higher
Power has dramatically shifted the way I think this year. I believe He
is training me to be more and more like Him. So, I guess when He
gives me a forgiving heart after my daughter is murdered and some
butterfly stories to share with the world, plants a seed in my pastor's
head telling him to connect me with Pat, and then Pat says you need
to write a book, I should probably listen and do that.

Who would have thought that the nation's leading expert in anything would attend our small church in Slinger, Wisconsin? You
never really know who people are when you meet them.

That can work both ways of course. Watching Dan play piano
with Jessie, you never would have known who he was either.

We should always remember when seeing others that we don't really know who they are, good or bad. Only the Almighty knows what's in their hearts, and what their path is.

Who knows what impact Pat's seminar will ultimately have. We'll find out. If The LOVE>hate Project can carry its message to schools around this country, it will be because of Pat and John.

I missed the status hearing because I chose to go to Consultant's Academy instead. It was a difficult choice, but it came down to this: the hearing was about the past. Learning to get into high schools and be a powerful voice for ending violence against women was about the future. That was one example of how my thinking was changing, and it was a total blessing.

Joy filled me in on the status hearing when I got home after the seminar. Not much of consequence had happened, with one notable exception: Judge Martens, at the State's request, had granted an exception to sequestration for Joy and me.

What that meant was Joy and I could sit in court and observe the whole trial. Under Wisconsin law, we would not have been able to observe the trial until after we testified, because we were subpoenaed as witnesses. We would have missed opening arguments and all proceedings until after we testified, or our subpoenas were released. It was possible that we could be called twice—once for our initial testimony, then again in the rebuttal phase later on. We could have missed much of the trial.

Once again, everything seemed so unfairly stacked against the victims and for the defendant. But Mark and Sandy, our D.A. and

Asst. D.A., along with Judge Martens, changed that. I guess that's pretty routine, but going through this for the first time one doesn't know what's routine. We worried about everything. Though I was now looking more forward than back, had we not been able to attend the trial, I think Joy and I would have gone crazy.

Dan's mom and dad were sequestered. I'm not sure how much of the early trial they missed. It must have been brutal for them, waiting outside in the hall for hours. Joy and I trusted them to tell the truth and not be influenced by witnesses ahead of them. We wished that they were also granted an exception to sequestration. But it wasn't our call.

The final thing that happened in that jam-packed first two weeks in July was that we rounded out our Board of Directors for the Project. I was on the Board along with Ian, Barb, and Laura. Their dedication and friendship thus far has been invaluable. You learn a lot about who your true friends are when life punches you in the gut. That's one of the beautiful things about hardship.

Bill Richards would be on our Board too. I met him through one of my patients, who had insisted upon it.

Bill grew up in a family that was always involved in nonprofit organizations. Supporting charities was so much a part of who he was that he attended Marquette University and earned a Master's Degree in Nonprofit Science. Who knew there was such a degree?

Bill was the expert and the legal guy we needed. We had the cause, the will, and the passion. But we didn't have the know-how. Becoming a legal nonprofit is not an easy endeavor. Bill knew every step of the path, every government form, and how to answer all the forms' questions so that it wouldn't get kicked back at you. He did all that mystifying paperwork for us. Bill gave me two great pieces of advice. First, he told me that in order to apply for nonprofit status, we needed a Board of Directors.

"You don't want a bunch of experts like me," he said. "You want people who are strongly connected to you, Jessie, and your cause."

Then, he said, "Watch out for mission creep."

"What the hell is mission creep?" I asked.

Bill said, "You're going to have a lot of input about what you should or shouldn't be doing, how to run your organization, and what your mission should be. You're going to have a lot of people donating money to your cause. Some will donate a lot. They'll want their opinions heard. You must define your mission and vision statements very clearly, and don't ever let anyone pull you off course."

Advice like that was exactly the reason we needed an expert.

I'm glad I said "yes" when my patient recommended I meet Bill. The old me wouldn't have. But the new me found that saying "yes" to life allowed me to see and enter the doorways that Providence presented.

I believe we are continually given possibilities. Try to see them. Knock and enter as often as you can.

So now we had our Board of Directors. There was Ian, representing and teaching us how to communicate with Jessie's generation. Barb, my childhood friend who had her own powerful survival story. Laura, who had given me Jessie's messages and taught anti-bullying classes. Bill, our expert. And me. Three of us were also Presenters. I love these people, Board and Presenters, and I love our mission.

And then…July 15, 2014 was upon us: the anniversary. No amount of love from others could cover this day. My excitement about the Project seemed a million miles away. Joy was a dark cloud that the sun could not penetrate, and so was I.

It was as if our happiness had fallen down a bottomless well with our girl. We could look down into the blackness hoping to see something. We could drop a stone and listen quietly as the seconds ticked by. But we would never hear a splash. Our happiness and our girl were too far away.

I forced myself throughout the day to look into Joy's eyes and try to comfort her, but her sorrow was so deep and her look so haunted I could barely keep eye contact.

I have no more words for this day and how it went. Language could never convey the primal sadness.

f Buck Blodgett

July 15, 2014

Jess, a year ago today....

At 12:35 p.m. I took the call from Mom. She had just turned you over to the first responders. She was sobbing, telling me she found you—you weren't breathing, you were blue, cold; there were marks on your neck. She did CPR, called 911. EMTs worked on you as we spoke. I asked if you were responding. She said "no." I asked if you were gone. No words came. I talked to God the whole drive home, hoping, praying. Our driveway was full—squad cars, firetrucks, ambulance, Crime Scene Unit vehicle. They wouldn't let me see you, touch you, hold you. Your room was taped off. I understood, but not being there for you when you needed help, or to say goodbye, was unbearable.

It's been a year of deep pain and profound Love. Never again will I take a single second of this life for granted. I was wrong about God and Spirit and life after death. You have gently and amazingly helped to open my eyes. You have infused some of yourself into me, made me kinder, braver, more musical, less tolerant of meanness and unfairness, but also less judgmental. I live for you now, sweetie, for your legacy, LOVE>hate. Mom and I miss you desperately. Of course nothing, even death, can break our bond and block our Love. See ya when I'm done here my hero, my brave and beautiful young woman.

TO ALL WHO LOVE JESS: she is HAPPY and FREE, and she wants the same for you TODAY and EVERY DAY.

I tried to hear my own words that day. Every other day, I could. But that day, the blackness was too thick.

chapter forty-six

TEA WITH MORIAH

"Let your heart guide you right along…"
—Jessie Blodgett, "Butterflies"

PERHAPS YOU REMEMBER MORIAH. SHE was escorting her summer camp kids down the street when Fire Chief Paul Stephens drove by in August of 2013, just weeks after Jessie's murder. She was the third "coincidence" of his lunch break, when plans for the community candlelight walk fell into place so easily.

Moriah was not only a good friend to Jessie; she was even closer to Dan. Imagine the mixed feelings of a young woman who had lost two friends this way. Who to support? Who to grieve for? How to make sense of it? The countless hours these three had spent together, traveling to Washington, DC on a school choir trip, working hard together and performing their hearts out in high school musicals, concerts, and state competitions…now one friend was gone and the other in jail charged with her murder.

On July 22, 2014, a year and a week since we lost Jess, Moriah and I met for tea at the Perc Place.

Moriah said, "I have something to share with you. About two weeks ago I got a call at work from my dad. There was a letter from the Washington County D.A.'s Office. Dad's tone suggested he might have thought it was some type of citation."

The dad in me thought that was understandable. When you get a letter from the D.A.'s office, it's probably not good.

She went on. "Dad apparently held the letter up to the light and saw Dan's name inside. He asked me if he could open it. I said no. I knew it was a subpoena."

Moriah was nervous to testify in front of Dan and his family. She had been friends not only with Dan, but with his older sister. I told her I was sorry for putting her in this situation. She told me it was her choice to talk to the D.A. and that she knew it was the right thing to do.

She said, "My dad asked if I wanted to talk about the subpoena, but I didn't want to. I wanted to think it over in my own private space. So I told Dad I had to go to Walmart after work, which I did.

"Driving alone in my car I was crying and thinking, trying to work through the feelings. I imagined myself testifying, facing Dan, facing his family, and facing your family. I pulled into a parking spot, turned off the ignition, and found myself talking to Jess.

"Then I composed myself, locked the car, and headed across the lot toward the front entrance. As I walked, still thinking about testifying and asking Jessie for guidance, something hit my shoulder, like a big bug. I hate insects, and this one landed on me. I raised my left hand, but before I swatted it I saw it was a beautiful monarch butterfly.

"I knew then Jess would be with me through all of this."

I thanked Moriah, and welcomed back the Great OKness.

chapter forty-seven

THE TRIAL

"But all you do is make me die…"
—Jessie Blodgett/Ian Nytes, "Love by Proxy"

AS BUSY AS THE FIRST half of July was, leading up to the anniversary, the second half passed like molasses sliding uphill.

The trial was coming in August. After a year of waiting, after the anemic pace of the legal process, after starting Jessie's project, and focusing on the future, I had mentally moved beyond it. But once the anniversary was behind us and August eleventh was on the horizon, I found my focus being pulled back.

The trial was coming, and I could barely wait.

Again, I wasn't waiting for vengeance, retribution, justice, or seeing Jessie's killer get his. I continued to mostly feel bad for Dan, to forgive him, and to pray for him. I'm not claiming that I never had basic human emotions. There were times when I was indescribably angry. I suspect there always will be. But those times took a major backseat to the presence of a profound and inexplicable Peace, Forgiveness, and Love.

Not the sadness and the emptiness, though—they were never in the backseat with anger. They were always in the front, battling with Peace, Forgiveness, and Love for the spotlight. Actually, the sadness and emptiness, in terms of sheer number of minutes, were clear winners last year. But the miraculous appearances of Love (when it showed up) were enough to carry me.

No, it was not justice or vengeance I couldn't wait for. It was truth. It was the chance to see all the facts come to light for the whole world to see. It was the chance to give Jess her voice back, and to see Dan, who had worked his cruelty in secrecy, have to face up to that truth in front of everyone who loved Jess, and everyone who loved him.

Waiting for the trial was hard, but Jessie's friends came to the rescue.

I rounded up a small group on short notice one day to shoot a video to anchor the homepage on the website.

Amelia and Jackie were our videographers. Like a lot of Jessie's friends, they had major artistic talent. Both appeared in the video too, with Amelia contributing the most emotional interview and Jackie closing it out. Jackie was free spirit incarnate, loud and fun and overflowing with enthusiasm—the perfect person to deliver a call to action.

Ian and Aaron appeared in the video, too, making strong statements like "Rape is NOT COOL" and "No Means NO." Aaron also edited an hour of film down to the best two minutes. Also in the video were Moriah, who called Jess her musical inspiration, Nancy, author of *Fuscia's Garden,* and Cody and Kelly, the last two friends to see Jess alive.

Well, except for Dan.

The video turned out great, and creating it kept me busy until the trial.

I didn't sleep well the night before the trial. I was too wound up. We waited thirteen months for this day. What would happen? How would it go? The case seemed open and shut to me, but Mark and Sandy taught us many things along the way, like you never know what kind of a jury you have until they make a decision.

I was nervous for Joy, who would testify early on. She was absolutely dreading it.

I was nervous for Jessie. I now believed that she was in a place where the petty workings of this world were powerless to affect the eternal grace of hers. Still, what would the Defense do? Would they continue with, "I wasn't there and I didn't do it"? Or would they do what Joy and I suspected and feared: change tactics during trial and claim a tragic accident had happened during a consensual bondage game, after which the defendant panicked?

We feared this tactic not because of anything the Defense had actually said or done, but because we couldn't imagine what other possible defense they could try.

If Dan used a tactic that attempted to smear Jessie's name after stealing her life, I swore to Joy—and Jessie—that I would crucify him in the press when the trial was over. I would let out the rage in words and destroy any shred of dignity and self-respect he had left. We knew this was no accident. And why do you bring a murder kit to an accident?

In times like that, when my mind was stuck in that place, I would always eventually hear the soft voice whisper things like, "Chill out. Rest in Me. Be patient. Let your anger and ego stand down. Look up, not down. Trust."

Sleep seemed hopeless deep into the night, but it finally took me.

I woke up before the alarm went off. Joy and I showered, made coffee, hopped in the van, and headed for the Washington County Courthouse. The family was there waiting on the concrete walkway. Many of Jessie's friends gathered inside, along with all the local news crews. Reporters were respectful and did not try to speak with us.

We passed together through the glass entrance way. This time there was a long line to security. The wide tiled hallway was bustling with people.

District Attorney Mark Bensen and Asst. D.A. Sandy Giernoth had explained in advance how today might go. First up was jury selection. Jury selection usually took an hour or so. In this case, however, they expected a much larger pool and a much longer process. It could be difficult to find people in Washington County who were not very familiar with this story, so roughly one hundred potential jurors had been called to duty to be sure that twelve unbiased and qualified jurors, plus two alternates, could be found. All of them had to be questioned in open court.

Mark explained that jury selection would probably take the whole morning session, 8:30 to noon, and likely even part of the afternoon too. Opening arguments would follow and last maybe an hour. If opening arguments were done by three o'clock, then the judge would instruct the State to begin calling witnesses. The first witness would be the 911 dispatcher. Her testimony would be short and straightforward—less than five minutes. Then, Mark would call Joy to the stand.

Because of the huge jury pool, we were told there might not be space in the courtroom and we might have to wait outside until jury selection was over. I was hoping we'd get in. I did not want to have to wait outside making small talk with friends and family when I was already on pins and needles. But Ali, Victim/Witness Coordinator, arranged seating for a small group of family and got us in.

After some initial obligatory proceedings, the judge called for the jury pool. One hundred potential jurors slowly filed in. Dan rose from his chair behind the Defense table. For the first time in over a year of hearings, he turned to face the gallery. He made eye contact with every juror, greeting them with a friendly smile.

My eyes jumped back and forth from Dan to the entering jury pool. How dare he put on an act for them now when he wouldn't look at me for a year. The anger deep within surfaced and burned red. For over a year we had endured complete silence out of the Defense, with no sign of remorse or acknowledgment. For over a year he avoided our eyes at all costs.

Now he was being friendly and open with the incoming jury pool.

I stared at him. I stared at him with a white-hot burning passion for Truth and Justice. My eyes burned holes right into his soul. I would neither accept nor tolerate this charade.

Despite the commotion of the whole jury pool passing between us, his gaze was pulled to mine. An instant of fear and then shame washed over him; he was busted, caught in the act. I know he felt my righteous wrath. His eyes went down, and from that moment on, try as he might, he could not restore his friendly, innocent countenance. He couldn't maintain steady eye contact with the entering pool for more than a second without sensing my stare and turning away.

Just as Love is stronger than hate, Truth is stronger than lies.

One by one, the judge called potential jurors. He queried each person as to their knowledge of this case, any biases they might have, and any relationship they might have with the defendant, the victim, their families, the legal teams, or anyone else involved.

One large man in the pool stated that he knew Jessie.

"Oh, my gosh," Joy whispered. "That's the dad who knocked on the door with Jessie's little piano student that day."

"My seven-year-old son took music lessons from Jessie. We came to the Blodgett house that day for his lesson. That's when Mrs. Blodgett found her," the man told the judge.

What a troubling and traumatic experience that must have been for that father. He was dismissed from jury duty.

Another woman knew Dan's mom from church. "They are such a good family. I can't believe her son could have done something like this."

When the judge asked her if she could find Dan guilty if the evidence showed him to be guilty beyond a reasonable doubt, she replied, "I don't think so."

This angered Joy. How could you not convict a killer if the evidence proved he did it? There were so many different sides to this whole thing, so many people affected in different ways. That potential juror was also dismissed.

The questioning of the jury pool went on all morning and into the afternoon. A few people just wanted out. A few more were deemed unfit for various reasons. But the overwhelming majority took their duty and their sacrifice of time and income very seriously.

By late afternoon, the whole pool had been processed by the judge. We had our "thirty in the box." These were the first thirty in line to serve. Now they would be questioned, again, by the Prosecution and the Defense. Each side could dismiss up to three jurors, so they had to choose wisely. The Defense dismissed a biologist who appeared perfectly qualified to sit on the jury. Apparently they didn't want a scientist explaining DNA evidence to other jurors.

Both sides skillfully questioned potential jurors to expose their biases. The judge held the pool accountable for their duty, while treating them with the utmost respect and courtesy.

It took until 5:00 p.m., but we had our jury.

We also had a heightened appreciation of the sanctity of the legal process in the United States—its assumption of innocence, its guarantee of rights, and the great responsibility of "a group of peers" to determine the defendant's fate. We understood the sacrifice these jurors were making—two weeks of work and income, two weeks of silence, even to their spouses, and living with the verdict for the rest of their lives.

Joy was emotionally exhausted. All day she waited, nervous about testifying. She hated public speaking, let alone having to relive her worst nightmare for all to see on network TV. She fretted about her hair, her outfit, and whether she would blank out on basic details, like the year Jess graduated, or her timeline the morning of July fifteenth. She worried that the defense attorney would try to make her look bad. She felt an overwhelming responsibility to do well for Jess.

My stomach churned for her all day.

Now she would have to endure yet another sleepless night. She would be even more tired and nervous. She would have to wait through opening arguments in the morning. I wished out loud that I could take this burden off her and testify in her place. But Joy was the one who found Jess and called 911. That was where the case started, the D.A. said, and only she could speak to this critical beginning.

At least we had our jury.

Tomorrow, we begin.

chapter forty-eight

OPENING ARGUMENTS

"Butterflies in my stomach,
Butterflies making me sick…"

—Jessie Blodgett, "Butterflies"

JOY WATCHED TV UNTIL 3:00 A.M. She couldn't sleep. I slept
fitfully. My mind was too keyed-up. It felt like I was running again in
the Boston Marathon, or the Packers were playing in the Super Bowl.
Those must sound like strange examples under the circumstances.
But the anticipation, despite the obvious tragic setting, gave me the
same nervous excitement.

For Joy it was more like dread. She felt the weight of being the
opening witness. She had been told that a good start was vital to a
trial. No one cared more about Jess than she did, and the State was
counting on her to make Jess real and tug on the heartstrings of the
jury. Coupled with being publicly grilled while asked to relive her

worst nightmare, in front of the world and TV cameras, it was a lot of pressure.

She woke up with her game face on. I could see it in her eyes. There was the purposeful inner strength that only a mother about to speak for her lost daughter could have. She didn't feel it yet. She was just exhausted and emotionally beat up. I sensed that when her time came, I would not want the defense attorney's job.

We grabbed our travelling mugs, poured in some French vanilla creamer, filled them to the brim with a steaming fresh Starbuck's medium roast, and hopped back in the van for the morning drive to the Washington County Courthouse.

"Please be seated," Judge Martens said upon entering the courtroom.

We learned that day to finish our coffee on the drive; they wouldn't let me bring my mug in. I was upset about that at first, but once inside the courtroom it didn't matter. I was ready.

Every session began with the gallery on our feet, showing respect for the judge, the Court, the process, and for the rule of law that civilized people understand is necessary for coexistence. I caught myself wishing that Dan would have shown some respect for the rule of law and Jessie's coexistence on that Monday morning in the summer of 2013.

"Is the State ready to present its opening arguments, Ms. Giernoth?"

"Yes, Your Honor."

Assistant District Attorney Sandy Giernoth rose from her chair behind the State's table. Sandy was tall with striking features. Her face emanated intelligence and goodness. She also glowed; Sandy was eight months pregnant.

Joy and I, and I'm sure Mark Benson, had prayed that she would make it through the trial without going into labor. She made her way toward the podium in front of the jury box.

Sandy's opening statement lasted about twenty minutes. This was the gist of it:

"Good morning, ladies and gentlemen of the jury. Thank you for sacrificing so much of your time, income, and energy to serve here today. I hope you had a good night's sleep.

"Over the next several days, you will see overwhelming evidence proving beyond a reasonable doubt that this man attacked Jessie Blodgett in her own bedroom while she was sleeping and intentionally murdered her.

"The State will show you, piece by piece, a mountain of undeniable physical evidence proving the defendant planned this attack and executed his plan. You will see the ligatures he used to bind and to strangle her. You will see the tape with her hair on it, which he used to gag ball her. You will see the cereal box that police found in the park containing these ligatures and tape, along with wipes used to clean up the scene."

The knot in my stomach tightened.

"You will see video that captured the defendant at this park with his backpack in the timeframe immediately after Jessie Blodgett was killed. You will see ligatures and tape matching the ones found in the cereal box that were found in the defendant's vehicle and residence.

"You will see blood evidence on bed sheets from Jessie's room, and more blood evidence on the wipes from the cereal box. You will hear an expert witness testify that DNA was found on the ligatures, the tape, and on Jessie herself. You will see that lab reports show that only two people's DNA were found on all these items—that of the victim, Jessie, and that of the defendant, that man sitting here in this courtroom."

Joy's hand held mine tighter. It was clammy. I leaned into her a little more.

"You will hear expert witness and police testimony about what was found in the defendant's computer after police confiscated it. You will hear about searches he had been doing prior to the victim's death. These searches will be dark and disturbing, searches of serial killers and their methods, searches of famous serial killers by number of victims, searches for the definition of spree killing."

I felt Joy's body quiver against mine as she sobbed silently.

"You will see a progression of witnesses from police and detectives to the coroner, the DNA expert and a computer expert. Their cumulative testimonies will prove beyond doubt the State's charge— the defendant planned and executed the intentional homicide of Jessie Blodgett.

"Now, the defense will plant seeds. They will try to cast doubt on what you will see and hear. They will do all they can to confuse and muddy the waters. They will bring up the issue of motive and claim there was none, despite the fact that Wisconsin law requires no motive, only proof of guilt.

"But they will give you no reasonable facts or arguments to explain the mountain of physical and DNA evidence against the defendant, nor a reasonable alternative explanation for Jessie's death. That's because there isn't one.

"It will therefore be your duty when proven beyond reasonable doubt that the defendant committed this first-degree intentional homicide to find him guilty. And you must do that. You must do that for Jessie. Thank you, ladies and gentlemen."

I was encouraged and optimistic. Sandy had laid a rock solid and clear foundation for what was to come. It looked as though, after having lived with the silence and unfairness of it all for so long, the Truth was indeed coming. The Light felt close now.

But my hopefulness was tempered. Joy was sitting close against me, and I could sense her anxiety. Her time was coming too.

Judge Martens thanked Ms. Giernoth, then said, "Mr. Schmaus, is the Defense ready to present its opening arguments?"

"Yes we are, Your Honor."

Attorney Gary Schmaus stood and moved to the podium. Mr. Schmaus was a sizeable man with a deep, pleasing voice and a relaxed, friendly demeanor. A seasoned veteran of the courtroom, he wore the lines of experience on his face. The D.A.'s office had warned me that I was taking him too lightly. Their respect for his ability was apparent.

Mr. Schmaus greeted the jurors like an old friend who was making them comfortable in his living room. He was warm, sincere, and casual, while being appropriately serious and grave over the circumstances that brought us all together.

If I were in his shoes, following Assistant District Attorney Giernoth's opening statement, I would have succumbed to my own thoughts that the jury and gallery would perceive me as the bad guy, a snake oil salesman defending a murderer. Mr. Schmaus seemed nothing of the sort. He was thoughtful, reasonable, and believable. Above all, he was likeable and commanding of respect.

He began.

"Hello ladies and gentlemen. Thank you for the important job you are about to do. Thank you for taking it so seriously.

"In our country we have a legal system that guarantees the presumption of innocence. The State has the burden to prove that my client is guilty of first-degree intentional homicide beyond any reasonable doubt. My client does not have to prove anything. He has no obligation to prove that he did not do this. He has no obligation to prove an alternative theory as to what actually happened. He has no obligation to prove anything at all.

"It is the State that must prove something. You will hear a lot of evidence and testimony over the next week or two. But you will see that there are many pockets of doubt throughout much of it. All we have to do is show that there exists some reasonable doubt as to the State's charges against the defendant. If we do that, then you must acknowledge that there is some reasonable doubt and you must find my client innocent."

While Defense Attorney Schmaus was delivering his opening statement, I panned back and forth from him to Dan to the jury for any sign of reaction. Dan sat impassive and poker-faced, except maybe for a very slightly up-curled lip, which my friends and family read as a smirk. The jury listened intently to every word from both the Prosecution and the Defense.

But as Mr. Schmaus advanced through the various things that the jury might hear about and see in the days to come, I could sense their demeanor change. He skillfully prepared them for the stunning facts to come, making points like "Stephen King writes dark novels, but that doesn't make him a criminal" and "authors, like Dan, will research their subject matter." He made every effort to take the shock out of such dark material, and paint it in a light of normalcy, as if it was something that we don't commonly talk about in society, but something that nonetheless occurs.

But there was nothing normal about it. Not in rural Washington County. When the jury heard there was evidence of searches involving sexual asphyxiation games and snuff films coming, their expressions visibly changed, especially the women.

The opening arguments were done in roughly an hour. The stage was set. Sitting next to me, Joy's anxiety was ramping up.

235

JOY TAKES THE STAND

"But I'm in love with a lie."
—Jessie Blodgett/Ian Nytes, "Love by Proxy"

"THANK YOU FOR YOUR OPENING statements," Judge Martens said. "Before we move now to the witness phase of the trial, let's take a fifteen-minute break."

My heart sunk. Joy's wait would be prolonged. She would have to go outside, hobnob with friends and family for a few more minutes, and worry some more. She would have to endure the thing she hated most—everyone and his brother coming up to wish her well. Everyone meant well, but she didn't want the attention.

I stayed close to her on this break, trying to be a shield and an encouragement. It seemed like an eternity before we finally reconvened.

Judge Martens addressed the court. "Before we bring the jury back and begin the next session, I need to make you aware that something has come up. One of the jurors has asked to be dismissed."

You're kidding, I thought. The first morning, and we are down to one alternate already? I had visions of going through a two-week trial, getting near the end, and then declaring a mistrial because we lost another juror or two to sickness or an emergency. What if we had to reschedule and start all over next year?

The judge continued, "She stated the subject matter in this case is too intense. She doesn't think she can handle it, and she asked to be relieved of her duties. I need some time to meet with her in chambers."

My heart broke for Joy. Are you kidding me? She had to worry about this trial for months. Then, she had to sit through an entire day of jury selection, waiting for her dreaded turn, which never materialized. Another sleepless night, waiting again through opening statements. Then the judge decides to take a break.... And now this; someone wants out, and the mother of the victim has to sit on pins and needles for God only knows how much longer. It was all too much.

Joy had to live through the rape and killing of her daughter and the stress of testifying. Now someone not even connected to Jess can't handle even listening to the facts?

But then I thought of that juror. She must have been terribly upset by the brutal nature of the crime, and also burdened by the heavy responsibility of determining the fate of a young man with no prior record.

This was becoming an issue for me in life now. How was it that I could forgive the man who killed my daughter, and yet be mad and irritated at people for little things, even things like this where they didn't really do anything wrong? I felt like God had given me amazing grace to get through several months of the shock phase. But that amazing grace period was fading now as I gradually slid back toward my normal human nature.

Why couldn't I maintain that grace?

Still, as the grace slowly faded, I was left with a permanent blessing, perhaps the most profound blessing of all. I was left with the indelible knowledge of what it was to forgive, love, and accept people unconditionally, regardless of what they had ever done or said, no matter how bad it was. I could never again completely forget the sacred sweetness of giving forgiveness when it wasn't deserved. And I now understood that I would have endless opportunities every day for the rest of my life to practice this habit. I would fail over and over again, but I would also succeed often, and get stronger and stronger at Unconditional Love.

It was clear that's what I was here for. That's what all of us are here for.

After twenty or thirty more minutes, the door to the judge's chambers opened.

"All rise."

The wait was over.

"I have had discussions with the juror in question, as has the State and the Defense. We are all satisfied that she is ready to proceed. Mr. Bensen, is the State ready to call its first witness?"

"Yes we are, Your Honor."

District Attorney Mark Bensen was a light-haired, handsome, middle-aged man of average height and build. He exuded integrity. His approach was soft-spoken and humble. Mark was the kind of man who grew on you. With every new meeting and conversation, I saw a little further into his character. On top of his experience and dedication, Mark was a dad with a great big heart.

Bensen called the 911 dispatcher to the stand. "Did you take an incoming call from Mrs. Blodgett on Wayside Drive in Hartford at 12:35 p.m. on Monday, July 15, 2013?"

"Yes, I did."

"Have you had the chance to listen to the recording of this call the State provided you? And is the recording an accurate depiction of the call that actually took place?"

"Yes I have, and yes it is."

"Did you instruct Mrs. Blodgett to perform CPR on her daughter that morning?"

"Yes."

"And did you dispatch emergency responders to the scene upon receiving that call?"

"Yes, I did."

The line of questioning was brief and routine, as Mark and Sandy said it would be.

"Thank you. No further questions, Your Honor."

The Defense had no substantial questions for the 911 dispatcher.

"Mr. Bensen, is the State ready to call its next witness?"

"Yes, Your Honor. The State calls to the stand Mrs. Joy Blodgett."

I felt my heartbeat. I whispered a final word of encouragement in Joy's ear as she rose from our bench to walk to the stand. I was nervous for her, but a peace came over me. Her wait was over. She would do fine. I knew it. All the months of thinking and stressing over this was what she hated. But now the time was upon her, and she would rise to the occasion, just like she always did for the patients in her office, just like her daughter did for every performance she ever had.

"Do you solemnly swear to tell the truth, the whole truth, and nothing but the truth?"

"I do."

District Attorney Bensen began. "Please state for the court your full name."

"Debra Joy Blodgett."

"Mrs. Blodgett, are you the mother of Jessie Blodgett?"

"Yes." Tears pooled in Joy's eyes.

"Mrs. Blodgett, did you come home that day, July 15, 2013, on a lunch break from work?"

"Yes, I did."

"What time did you come home?"

"Well, my office computer showed that I logged off at 12:20, which is the last thing I do before I walk out the door. It just takes me a few minutes to drive home, so I believe I arrived home about 12:25.

"And what did you do when you arrived home?"

"Well, I started to make lunch, and I called up to Jess. She didn't answer. I thought she was just sleeping in, because she had three *Fiddler on the Roof* performances on Friday, Saturday, and Sunday, and a cast party until late Sunday night. Plus, it was the first Monday of summer vacation that she didn't have to get up early to teach the kids in the summer school orchestra program.

"As I was making lunch, a dad and his young son knocked on our door, for a 12:30 music lesson. So I called up to Jess. She didn't answer."

Joy took a breath.

"I got mad at her for not being ready for her lesson." Joy was sobbing. "I ran upstairs to wake her up, but she wasn't responding, and I couldn't understand why."

You could see the bewilderment and shock in Joy's face even thirteen months later as she reflected back on this scene that will be forever burned into her memory.

"I walked over to her bed, and I touched her to wake her up. She was cold."

The word "cold" left her mouth and hung in the air.

I looked over to Dan as Joy spoke. His face seemed blank and devoid of emotion to me, as if he was watching TV.

Joy went on. "I rolled her over, and she was blue. There were tiny red dots all over her face and in her eyes. I immediately picked up the phone on her nightstand and called 911."

District Attorney Bensen took over. "I want to play for the court the recording of the call that Mrs. Blodgett made to the 911 dispatcher that day. The call is a little over four minutes long."

The recording began with the phone ringing, then Joy's voice in what I can only describe as controlled hysteria:

"Oh, my God. Oh, my God!"

"Hartford 911," the dispatcher answered.

"My daughter is blue. I just got home from lunch, and I went to wake her up. She won't wake up!"

"How old is your daughter?"

"Nineteen. Oh, my God! Oh, my God!"

"Nineteen? Okay. Hang on just a second (silence). Is she breathing?"

"No, I don't think so."

"Not breathing? …Oh…."

241

"I don't think so. She's blue. I tried to wake her up and she's not waking up!"

"Okay, alright, hang on, ma'am."

Joy's sobbing filled the spaces between their words.

"Okay, ma'am, we're going to try CPR, alright? Do you know how to do CPR?"

"Jessie! Jessie!" Joy was wailing now.

"Ma'am, do you know how to do CPR?"

"She's cold! She's cold!"

"She's cold?" the dispatcher repeated.

"She's cold! Oh, my God!"

"She's cold," the dispatcher repeated again, to a third party on her end.

"Oh, my God …Oh, my God …Oh, my God."

"Ma'am, stay on the line with me, we're going to get EMS out for you." Again, to an unknown third party, she says, "She's cold to the touch and she's blue."

Joy continued, "Her pants are all wet…and it looks like…she's got…" Joy said in disbelief, "strangulation marks…."

The call continued on for three more minutes. You could hear Joy performing CPR and pleading with Jess. At one point she asks, "Jessie, Jessie, what happened to you?"

When the recording ended the whole room sat for several long seconds in a numb silence.

I had not heard this call before. It launched me back instantly to the moments of Joy's phone call to me at my office thirteen months prior.

I glanced down the front row of the gallery, found my mom, Jessie's grandma, with tears running down her cheeks.

District Attorney Bensen guided Joy through the remainder of his line of questioning. He had her describe the events during and following that 911 call, right up through the arrival of police and first responders, to when Jessie was pronounced dead, and her room was taped off and declared a crime scene. It was then that Jess changed from being her daughter to being evidence, a ward of the State.

Joy's description of these events as they unfolded was critical, because the Defense would try to cast doubt on some of the circumstances of the crime scene. Joy answered every question seamlessly and transparently. She did a great job.

"No further questions, Your Honor."

"Thank you, Mr. Bensen," the judge said. "Mr. Schmaus, does the Defense have questions for this witness?"

"Yes we do, Judge."

"Please proceed."

"Thank you, Judge."

Defense Attorney Schmaus slowly approached the bench, keeping a cushion of distance from Joy. This would be tricky. If he was insensitive to the grieving mother of a murder victim, if he appeared in any way to be too hard on her or to attack her, he could lose this jury fast and hard.

Not only was he soft-spoken, patient, and courteous, he seemed genuinely kind and understanding.

But today, in this courtroom, the Defense Attorney was a villain to our side. He was a reprehensible figure. He was someone who had no conscience and no morals, someone who would say or do anything to defend a man who he must know in his heart killed our Jessie. He was someone who would try to deny Jessie justice, in order to win a case.

But the Great Healer was working on me again, gently teaching me that my perceptions were once again false, reminding me that only He knows all of what is in the heart and mind of a man.

Mr. Schmaus was also one of His children. Who was I to judge? What did I know about his path? In fact, he had taken on an extremely difficult job, defending people accused of heinous crimes. You had to be a strong person to perform this unpopular task that was so essential to the freedom and human rights our great country enjoys.

Attorney Schmaus began, "Mrs. Blodgett, I'm very sorry for your loss."

It seemed to me he meant that. My family disagreed.

"Mrs. Blodgett, when you moved Jessie from her bed to the floor that day to administer CPR, can you describe for us how you accomplished that?"

The Defense Attorney proceeded with Joy through a line of questioning designed to create some doubt about the handling of the crime scene prior to and after the arrival of the police.

Joy did great in answering his questions. She never stumbled, contradicted herself, or appeared at all confused.

He was masterful at uncovering a tiny seed of doubt here, and another there, at every possible point along the line. His tone almost magically suggested doubt, even when there really wasn't any. The D.A. was right. Mr. Schmaus was very good at his job.

He cross-examined Joy for about half an hour. He pursued several different lines of questioning, all the while adding pebbles of doubt wherever and whenever he could, running every line to its completion, searching everywhere for holes.

Joy gave him very little of substance.

At one point, he asked about Dan's visits to our home in the weeks preceding Jessie's death. He seemed to be trying to establish that Dan was welcome in our home, and a friend of the family.

"After Dan dropped out of college, did he come to your home?"

"Yes, he did."

"What did he and Jessie typically do there?"

Was he hoping that Joy wouldn't know?

"Well, he came over three times I believe. Each time, they were in Jessie's music room, by our front entrance, where she taught lessons."

"How long was he usually over for?"

"They usually played and sang, and wrote songs, for maybe an hour or so."

"Did you see him each time he came over?"

"Usually, but not always. One time I walked in the front door and they were already there playing and singing. That was the time that Dan whispered something to Jessie."

"What do you mean?"

"Well, as I came in the door, I saw him whisper something in her ear. Then Jess said, 'Yeah. Mom, aren't you home early?' So I knew that's what Dan had whispered to her."

Joy had led Attorney Schmaus exactly into one of the points that she had hoped to make in court.

Since Jessie's death, that incident had bothered Joy. Looking back, Dan was inquiring into Joy's work schedule and timeline. She told the D.A., but Mark and Sandy advised us that they could not ask Joy about that in the trial, because that would be "hearsay" under Wisconsin law.

Hearsay meant Joy could not testify as to something Jessie told her, because the Defense would have no chance to cross-examine

Jessie about what was said, since Jessie was dead. Once again, all the protections seemed to be for the perpetrator and not the victim.

But Joy, as nervous and tired and emotionally drained as she was, had the presence of mind to steer the Defense right into letting her make that point about Dan.

It wasn't Attorney Schmaus's fault. It wasn't that he made a mistake. It was Dan's fault. Dan made the great mistake that he had been making for thirteen months. He was living a lie.

He didn't even tell his own attorney about Joy catching him questioning her schedule. So his attorney, having no knowledge of what to look out for, walked right into Joy's trap in which she got to bypass the hearsay law and tell the truth, just by responding to his question.

Funny how the Truth works.

Abraham Lincoln said the good thing about always telling the truth is you don't have to remember anything.

Apparently Dan had too much to remember.

Incidentally, the biggest part of Dan's big mistake, living a lie, is he cut himself off from God. When we lie we separate ourselves from the Truth. God is Truth. And He is also Forgiveness and Love.

When we lie, we separate ourselves from Truth, Forgiveness, and Love, because God is all those things. He will never force us to behave, because He will never violate His most sacred gift to us: free will. He will wait patiently, forever if need be, until we by our own free will choose to come back to Him, choose to return to Truth, Forgiveness, and Love, like the prodigal son returned to his father, who accepted him back with open arms.

Schmaus dropped that line of questioning like a hot potato and picked up a different one. He moved on smoothly, hoping, I think, that the jury would miss what had just happened. I'm sure some did, but in a group of twelve, someone was sure to bring that up in their private discussions later on. Joy had scored her point and the damage was done.

"Mrs. Blodgett, let's talk for a minute about the vigil at your house."

"Sure."

"This was the day after Jessie passed, when all her best friends came over to support you, is that right?"

"Yes, yes it was."

"How many people were at your house that day?"

"Maybe twenty," Joy replied.

"And were they mostly Jessie's friends, or your family, or neighbors, or who?"

"Our families hadn't arrived from out of town yet. It was all Jessie's friends."

"Who was over at your house that day?"

Joy began to name Jessie's best friends.

"Was Dan at your house that day?"

"Yes, he was."

"Do you know who he came with?"

"Yeah, I think he came with Ian and Davis, two of Jessie's close friends."

"And do you remember how long he was there for?"

"I think he was with us for about three hours."

Mr. Schmaus seemed pleased. Dan was known to be a good actor. He always got leading roles in the school and local musicals. But

247

if he was guilty, a kid would have to be the actor of the century to show up at the home of his victim the day after killing her and spend three hours crying with her family and best friends. His line of questioning, establishing Dan as a family friend and someone who was present in our home recently, which maybe could explain the presence of DNA evidence, seemed to be progressing well. He was about to close it out.

"And do you recall when Dan left the vigil at your house, Mrs. Blodgett?"

"Yes, I do."

"Was it early evening, when he got the call from the Slinger Police Department asking if he would come in and answer some questions?"

"Yes, it was. He seemed a little unnerved or upset. I asked him what was wrong. He told me that the Slinger Police wanted to question him, something about mistaking his vehicle for someone else's."

Joy knew that she couldn't talk about the attack in Richfield Park, because the two cases had been separated. "I tried to reassure him. I said, 'Don't worry, Dan, the police will want to question all of Jessie's friends. It's just routine. You and Jess dated years ago, and they'll just want to ask you some questions.' He seemed a little scared, and all these young kids were all going through this terrible ordeal with us, and I just wanted to support him."

Then Defense Attorney Schmaus asked, "Is that when Dan left then?"

"Yes, right after I thanked him for talking with Jess about the kiss."

"The what?"

"The kiss. The kiss he had given her at his house—against her will."

Schmaus's face appeared to tighten.

Joy went on before he had a chance to redirect. "Jess was at his house singing and playing in his music room a few weeks before she died. She came home and told me and her dad that Dan had completely, unexpectedly, and out of the blue, grabbed her by the hips and pulled her in for a kiss. She told us she pushed him away and scolded him for it, told him he had a girlfriend, and asked him what the hell he was doing. Later, they talked about it. He apologized and told Jessie he had been making a lot of bad choices lately."

There was nothing Schmaus could do to stop her story now without appearing that he was trying to hide something.

"Jess was satisfied with his apology," Joy continued. "It actually opened the door for them to talk about aspects of their breakup years earlier they never really talked about. So I wanted to thank Dan for doing that."

The D.A. could not ask Joy about the "kiss against Jessie's will" for the same reason he couldn't ask about the whisper: hearsay law. But Schmaus had asked Joy about Dan's attendance at our vigil, and not knowing about the kiss, he walked right into it. Again.

Once again, Dan had been too busy living a lie and separating himself from Truth to remember to tell his attorney this piece of information.

Being separate from Truth can sure sabotage a person.

I once heard sin defined this way: it isn't the committing of a terrible wrong. It's simply a lack of Love, a separation from God. I've always liked that definition of sin. There's no judgment in it.

The opposite of sin, then, the opposite of being separated from God, is simply atonement, which is Old English for at-one-ment, or the condition of being united with God.

I was so proud of Joy. I could barely contain my happiness. She had stressed and worried, missed sleep, and suffered from anxiety for months over this day. She feared messing up times and numbers; she worried about misrepresenting Jessie, about not communicating "her goodness" effectively to the jury. Not only did Joy represent our daughter wonderfully, she managed to get two key points in, as well. She knocked it out of the park.

Nothing will shine Light in the darkness like the love of a mother for her departed daughter.

THE ROPE

"Gotta teach 'em,
Make 'em get it straight…"

—Jessie Blodgett, "Overnight"

AFTER THIRTEEN MONTHS OF HELL, waiting for our day in court, and waiting to reclaim Jessie's silenced voice, the trial had begun in spectacular fashion.

Thanks to opening arguments, the 911 call, and then Joy's dramatic testimony, the truth was starting to come out for all to see.

We took a lunch break. My whole family and Joy's brother's family from Canada went to a local restaurant and talked over every detail of the morning's events.

Everyone told Joy what an amazing job she did.

Next up would be Sergeant Joel Clausing from the Washington County Sheriff's Department, followed by Detective Rich Thickens from the Hartford Police Department. The State had decided to lay out their case chronologically, as it happened. That's why they began with the 911 operator and Joy's testimony. Now they would move to the police investigation phase.

Testimony by Clausing and Thickens took up the rest of that Tuesday and most of Wednesday. Both officers were prepared, strong, and articulate. They performed like pros.

During the investigation, they did everything right. They investigated all leads to completion, despite feeling early on that they had their man. No one could say later they zeroed in on a suspect and ignored other possibilities. They were thorough and smart, attending to every detail. They handled all evidence and their suspect by the book, respecting his rights and leaving no opening for him to get off on a technicality.

District Attorney Bensen and Assistant D.A. Giernoth questioned the officers, starting with the crime scene in Jessie's bedroom; to the interviews of Dan the next two days; to the search of Woodlawn Park, where the cereal box full of ligatures, tape, hair, and blood-stained wipes was found on Thursday; to the search warrants executed on Dan's vehicle and home; to the handling of all the physical evidence as it went to and from the State Crime Lab.

No physical evidence had been touched without using fresh latex gloves, and all of it had been sealed in evidence bags to avoid cross contamination of DNA.

I was so impressed with how these men, who could not have had much experience with murder investigations during their careers in Washington County, conducted themselves.

The trial progressed through several more witnesses. There were a couple more police officers. There was the Human Resources Manager at the company where Dan originally claimed to be working when Jess was killed. She testified that Dan had never worked one day there, let alone for several months, like he had told family, friends, and police.

There was our neighbor, Bethany, from up the cul-de-sac. Bethany was young and innocent. She babysat for Jessie when Jess was little. It must have been horrible for her to have to testify at Jessie's murder trial.

Bethany saw Joy's blue van parked in our driveway when she entered our neighborhood at 8:00 a.m. on July 15, 2013. Joy would leave for work just minutes later. Bethany also observed a blue van in a different spot at the top of our driveway as she left the neighborhood around 10:00 a.m. We knew that van was not Joy's, and her description matched Dan's van.

And then there was Dan's own mother. District Attorney Bensen subpoenaed her to testify for the State. In a stunning display of courage and integrity, she took the stand and answered every question honestly.

She acknowledged straight out that her son, who she so deeply loved, lied to her for months while pretending to go to a job he never had. She even acknowledged that he, in fact, had a long history of not telling the truth.

Watching her sit in front of us all, in front of the whole world, and tell such an impossibly difficult truth, I wondered how Dan could have missed the value of honesty that was so strong in his mom.

At one point the D.A. asked Dan's mom about his parents' expectation for him to get a job.

She stated simply, "Well, yeah, if you drop out of college and come back home to live, you are expected to get a job."

Joy later told me that she saw Dan's face visibly change when his mom said this. Joy thought his expression changed from a little boy who loved his mom to being mad at her for holding him accountable for something.

Later in the week, the State called Debra Kaurala, the DNA expert from the Wisconsin State Crime Lab. She testified in plain English what DNA is, how it is tested, the sampling process, the concept of cross-contamination, how DNA material is extracted from objects, and how it is handled so as to prevent contamination.

She explained that the semen material found in Jessie's vaginal cavity was of a quality that would not allow exact identification to one specific person. This DNA, however, could be positively identified to a sub-category of DNA that only one in thirty-five hundred people would match.

I did the math. There were about fourteen thousand people in Hartford as of 2013. If half of them were male, that leaves seven thousand boys and men. In other words, out of all the boys and men in the whole town of Hartford, only two would match this category of DNA.

Assistant D.A. Giernoth led the State Crime Lab DNA expert through questions that revealed far more compelling data.

"Were you able to extract DNA from the ligatures that you see in the exhibits before you?"

"Yes, we were."

"Can you describe for us where the DNA extractions came from?"

"Sure, we were able to extract high quality DNA from several materials like the ligatures, the hair, the gag ball, the wipes, the tape, and also from under the victim's fingernails. We could only get a lower quality sample from the semen. We also obtained DNA from the blood on the sheets."

"Was one of those materials the thick rope you see in the Exhibit before you?"

(This thicker rope was the ligature that the coroner would later say was a perfect match with the strangulation markings on Jessie's neck.)

"Yes, we extracted high quality DNA from that particular thicker ligature."

"Can you describe for the jury where on this rope you extracted DNA from?"

"We extracted DNA from three locations on the rope, from each end, and also from the middle."

"Can you tell us about the quality of this DNA?"

"These DNA samples were high quality, and we could compare them much more precisely with the DNA samples from the victim and the defendant."

"And what did you find? Did the DNA extracted from the ligatures match the DNA from the sample provided by the defendant?"

"Well, you can't definitively say DNA belongs to someone. That's not how DNA works. What we can say is that the DNA samples from the ligatures and from the defendant correlated so completely that the odds that someone else could have the same correlation are about sixty quadrillion to one."

Holy smokes. Sixty quadrillion to one. The Light was shining ever brighter into the darkness.

I couldn't help myself; I did the math again. There are roughly seven billion people on our planet. A trillion is a thousand billion. A quadrillion is another thousand of those. Therefore, the odds that there was even just one other person on this entire planet whose

DNA could match the DNA from the ligatures like Dan's DNA did were roughly nine million to one. In other words, it would take a thousand galaxies, each with nine thousand planet Earths in them, with seven billion people on each "Earth," to find one other person that might match the DNA found on this ligature.

Still saying you weren't there and you didn't do it?

I remembered back to opening statements when Defense Attorney Schmaus discussed the fallibility of science. That contention wasn't looking too good by the time Debra Kaurala finished testifying.

"And Ms. Kaurala," Sandy continued, "Can you tell us where on the rope you extracted these samples that correlated so strongly with the defendant's DNA?"

"The DNA extractions that correlated with the defendant's DNA came from both ends of the rope."

"And did you also find DNA in the middle of the rope?"

"We did. The DNA extraction that came from the center of the rope had an equally strong correlation with the DNA sample from the victim, Jessie Blodgett."

There it was. The picture could not have been painted much clearer. Dan had held both ends of the rope. The middle of it went around our daughter's precious neck.

DNA was found on nearly every item in the cereal box. It was always from Dan, or Jessie, or both; no one else's DNA was found. Defense Attorney Schmaus did his best to portray a box that had sat outside in the weather for three days, mixed together with all kinds of other refuse in the garbage can. It had been rained on. His questioning showed how detectives must have had to dig through all that stuff and touch it all. He portrayed the whole mess as a fertile ground for cross-contamination.

But the basic facts remained, and there was not much he could do about them. The cereal box's contents were loaded with DNA, and it was from two people and two people only.

Parts of the trial were difficult to sit through, especially when we heard something new. We thought going in that we knew everything there was to know. We were wrong. Occasionally, some new little detail would emerge. Each detail added to the picture of what Jess went through. Each new fact enhanced our understanding of what she must have felt or thought, and the pain and the terror she must have experienced.

Joy and I leaned against each other often. I held her hand during many tough parts. Some testimony was graphic and vivid, and I would wrap both arms around her. I also worried, along with my siblings, about my eighty-four-year-old mom. She sat through every minute of this, as did my eighty-five-year-old dad.

On breaks, and on Facebook, many people said they were sorry we had to relive the whole thing. Honestly, for both of us, we relived it every day, all day. How could one not think constantly about their lost child after such an event?

Despite how intense it was, for me, the trial was cathartic more than anything. It was the Truth coming out. It was the Light being turned on. It was everyone we cared about finally knowing what we'd known all this time.

chapter fifty-one

THE CORONER

"All I need,
All I want,
Is everything you have."
—Jessie Blodgett/Ian Nytes, "Love by Proxy"

THE DAY CAME FOR THE Coroner to testify. The State called Waukesha County Medical Examiner Dr. Lynda Biedrzycki to the stand. Dr. Biedrzycki was on loan to Washington County for this high profile case because she was the best around. As with every witness, the State began by establishing her credentials.

"Dr. Biedrzycki, you're a licensed and Board Certified medical doctor in the State of Wisconsin, correct?"

"Yes, I am."

"Where did you get your medical degree from, Doctor?"

"I received my medical degree from Harvard University School of Medicine."

"And do I understand that you have also trained other medical examiners in techniques and curricula pertaining to forensic science?"

"Yes, I have."

"And where did you teach, Doctor?"

"Also at Harvard University."

Dr. Lynda Biedrzycki looked smart just sitting there, and she sounded even smarter when she opened her mouth. This lady's photo was in the dictionary next to brilliant.

With every other witness, Defense Attorney Schmaus reviewed their credentialing, always finding minute details here and there to slightly degrade their status, even the DNA expert and the police officers. It wasn't easy; these were highly professional, well-trained, fully credentialed people. But Schmaus had a job to do, and he was excellent at it. He took everyone down a notch or two and showed that they were not their big degree, but rather just regular people doing big jobs.

But when it was time to cross-examine Dr. Biedrzycki, Schmaus skipped right over the credentials' review. He recognized brilliance when he saw it, and he knew this medical examiner's qualifications were so far beyond question that to do so would only damage the Defense's believability.

Joy tilted her head against mine and whispered, "How fitting that the smartest person in the room is a woman. Jessie would be proud."

It was a trial dominated by brilliant women, from Harvard-trained Dr. Biedrzycki to Assistant D.A. Sandy Giernoth, to the DNA and computer experts, to even the HR Director and the two mothers whose testimonies were powerful and compelling.

Dan's mom, by the way, is an accomplished violinist. And Joy is a doctor herself, running her own clinic for eighteen years now.

This fact was not lost on us, nor do I believe it was lost on Jess, whose presence I felt in court that week. Male against female sexual violence is very often an act of control, dominance, and humiliation, an act of using physical force and sex to put a victim "in her proper place." That's different from a crime of passion. Sandy, the Assisant D.A., would be quoted in the paper after the trial saying: *"...To inflict this type of crime on her was an act to shame her, desecrate her body."*

Now, it was coming full circle. Now, the sick and twisted mind was being put in its proper place, exposed in plain view for all who could stand looking at it, and the lion's share of the exposing was being done by women. Women were standing tall and strong in Jessie's trial. Somewhere, in some form and place incomprehensible from here, she was proud.

Dr. Biedrzycki had a knack for reducing complexities to common language and for seamlessly bridging the gap between her knowledge and a layperson's. It is one thing to be brilliant; it is quite another to share your insight at a user-friendly level.

"Your Honor," said D.A. Mark Bensen, "I would now like to display the series of crime scene photos on the projector for the jury to see, as we previously discussed."

We had spent an hour the prior day, with the jury excused from the room, reviewing dozens of graphic photos. The defense had argued against showing most, calling them inflammatory and unnecessary. They could bias the jury against the defendant due to their emotional nature. Many photos, usually the most graphic ones, were ruled out during this process, but some were allowed so the prosecution could use them to illustrate the coroner's testimony.

"I will grant the State permission to display briefly, for discussion purposes, the approved photos. I want to advise the gallery beforehand as to their graphic nature. It is my understanding that the family condones the use of these images and chooses to remain in the room while they are shown."

Throughout the trial, Judge Martens refrained from making much personal eye contact with the gallery. But he was looking right at Joy and me now. His eyes seemed those of a father, not a judge. He wanted to be sure that while he was ensuring a proper and fair trial for the accused, he was also not adding harm to a family already traumatized by tragedy. He was giving us fair warning to get up and go now if we had changed our minds.

We had not. I imagined he could not quite fathom the strength of a mother to sit and observe these photos of her deceased daughter. Nobody seemed to be able to. But they could not understand as Joy did that no photo could ever compare to the real life image forever seared into her brain. She found Jess, after all. If her mind had the chance to grow old and senile, and all her memories faded into oblivion, and eventually she forgot even me, I believe this memory would still remain.

The projector screen came to life.

"Dr. Biedrzycki, do you recognize this photo?"

"Yes, we took it in the Waukesha County medical examiner's office."

That was a euphemism for the morgue.

"Can you describe the photo for us and tell us what the purpose of taking it was, please?"

The photo was a close up of Jessie's wrists. It did not show her face and body. The judge would allow only one photo showing her face and body for explanatory purposes. Anything else he ruled unnecessary and inflammatory.

261

"We took this photo to document the ligature marks on her wrists. Notice the angle of the marks. We placed her arms and hands in various positions trying to understand how these markings could be angled like this. When we crossed one wrist over the other and placed ligatures replicating the smaller ones found in the cereal box around her wrists, we found that the ligatures would have left these exact markings."

The D.A. put the next photo up on the screen. Joy snuggled a little closer against me.

"Dr. Biedrzycki, do you recognize this next photo?"

"Yes, this one we took to document the ligature markings on her ankles. Notice that these markings are not angled. They are more horizontal. When we placed her ankles together, but didn't cross them, we found that the ligatures that were exact replicas of the ones found in the cereal box also matched these markings.

"Notice also that there are markings on the outside of each ankle, but not the inside. That's because, if the ankles were placed together and bound tightly, there would be no ligature contact on the insides of each ankle, but the bindings would be tightest here on the outside, which is why the markings are worse there."

Next came close up photos of Jessie's knees and elbows. Joy leaned in further. We had not seen all these pictures before. They were protected evidence. We wanted to see them. We needed to see them. We needed to understand *everything*. But still, as every new image added clarity to the picture, that meant renewed shock and deeper heartbreak.

"What about these pictures, Doctor?"

"These side-by-side photos are of the victim's knees and elbows. Notice the deep bruising and abrasions on all four surfaces. These bruises were not visible in the photos of her lying on her bedroom floor just hours after she died. We took these to document the injuries, which became more apparent the next day.

"See all the pooled blood? Notice the road rash on each joint surface. This is clearly indicative of how hard she tried to move, to roll herself over, and to lift herself up. If your hands and feet are bound, and someone is on you, then when you are on your back you must drive yourself up on your elbows when trying to rise. If you're face down with feet and hands bound, you must try to push up from your knees.

"These injuries are obvious signs of struggle. She fought hard in an attempt to move, roll over, and get up."

I had wrestled with anger surprisingly little during the past thirteen months, but I was wrestling with it now. Still, this was exactly what we had hoped to hear from the coroner. We feared a defense of "tragic accident," consensual sex gone wrong, followed by panic and an unfortunate lie. Dr. Biedrzycki was leaving little doubt about her opinion: this was no accident.

Earlier in the trial the Defense spent a lot of time reviewing the crime scene. Attorney Schmaus grilled the police officers about the lack of signs of a struggle. They were forced to admit that the room looked like that of a typical teenager. (They had all chuckled while testifying about "messy Jessie's" room. But no one thought it was messy because of a struggle or fight.)

We all knew why. Dan surprised her while she was sleeping. D.A. Bensen and Assistant D.A. Giernoth both highlighted that Dan was over two hundred pounds at the time of Jessie's death, and Jess only weighed about one hundred and fifteen pounds. There was no sign of struggle in the room because Jess never had a chance to get out of bed and fight back. Dan had lost a fight in the park to a woman half his size three days earlier. He made sure his next target wouldn't have a fair chance to fight back.

Next we were shown photos of Jessie's back, sheets, face, and tongue. There was a large bruise on her mid back. I imagined her face down, bewildered, waking up to Dan's attack. He was on top of her binding her hands with his knee firmly planted in my little girl's spine. He was wrenching her arms behind her, hurting her shoulders. I never asked the coroner if she examined Jessie's rotator cuffs. I was afraid I would learn they had been torn.

Her sheets showed over a dozen small bloodstains. One stain by her feet was likely from after she died, when Dan cut the ligatures from her ankles to remove the evidence. The State asserted that he must have nicked her leg when cutting the ropes.

The remaining small stains were where her elbows and knees likely would have been pressed into the bed during her struggle. Another stain was probably from where the thick rope bit so deeply into her neck. And a larger one had likely pooled under her tongue.

The close-up photo of her tongue was the hardest one for me to take. It showed my girl's tongue wedged against her teeth and the side of her face. She had bitten clear through it.

My heart cried. Love *is* greater than hate, but humans are imperfect, and I am human. It was at this point I wanted to kill Dan.

It was a primal feeling, the heated lust to kill, pure animal instinct, no right or wrong. Is this what killers felt? But I would feel no pleasure in killing him, in dominating and humiliating him. Basic animal instinct may be to kill, but it takes evil to enjoy it, to revel in the victim's degradation and pain.

There really wasn't a lot of blood, thank God. Jessie would have been more terrified to see herself bleeding all over. She hated the sight of it. But the multitude of milder injuries—the ligature markings, the abrasions on her knees, elbows, and back, the biting of her tongue—all added up to one fierce fight-for-your-life struggle.

My crying heart was proud of her. I just wanted to cuddle her in my arms and tell her it was OK now. But I knew that where she was she was wrapped in far better arms than I could ever provide. In fact, she was comforting me now. She was with Love Himself. A butterfly had shown me that.

I would not have believed that fourteen months ago. And I would not believe it now just because I needed or wanted to. I believed that now because she, and He, answered my prayers and made it clear to me, over and over.

"Your Honor, we just have one final photo to show. This is the image showing the ligature markings to Jessie's neck. We will only put it up briefly, as agreed on, but this photo is very relevant to intent and to Dr. Biedrzycki's explanation of her determined cause of death."

"Proceed."

The photo went up. A collective gasp broke the courtroom silence. I watched the faces of the jurors. It seemed most had not seen death before, or at least not a shocking death of one so young.

"Can you please describe this photo, Doctor, and explain what it tells us?"

"Of course. This is the wider ligature marking on the victim's neck. In my office, I placed the replica climbing rope that detectives purchased to match the one found in the cereal box next to the victim's neck. Observe the pattern on the rope. Compare it to the dotted and lined ligature mark on the neck. Notice how the pattern

265

on the neck is exactly the kind of marking that such a patterned rope would cause, and the width of the marking matches the width of the rope as well.

"Notice there is a single wide band where the rope was held against the victim's neck. There are no secondary or multiple markings, just one clear and distinct band. This tells us that once in place, the rope never moved. This, to me, is evidence that the rope was held tightly and forcefully in place, so much so that no slippage was ever allowed, or else we would see markings in other places.

"Now look at all the little red dots on the victim's face. They are all over her eyes too. These are petechiae. Petechiae are exploded blood vessels. They burst from a lack of oxygen to the head, face, and eyes. This takes total and sustained oxygen starvation.

I wondered how much it hurt while all those little blood vessels were exploding.

I prayed the Elton John song Jess sent me via Laura Gruber to answer my question, *What do you want me to know about your passing, sweetie?* was true. I prayed that *someone saved her life*...that morning, that *sweet Freedom whispered in her ear*, and said, *"Butterflies are free to fly, fly away...."* I prayed she flew away before all those little blood vessels burst.

"In the lab, we incised the neck muscles underneath the strangulation marks. I have seen many strangulation marks in my career as a medical examiner. I have seen few more severe than these.

"We incised the muscles to look at them. There are three layers of muscles in the front of our necks. These are called the anterior strap muscles. When we exposed the outer layer, there was clear and significant hemorrhaging of the muscle. It was badly injured.

"When we exposed the middle layer of anterior neck muscles, there was also significant hemorrhaging of this muscle. It, too, was badly injured.

"And, finally, we exposed the deep layer of muscle in the front of the neck. This layer is so deep that it lies directly against the spine. This layer of muscle was significantly hemorrhaged as well, more so than in most strangulations. In summary, all three layers of muscle in the victim's neck were hemorrhaged and injured right to the spine."

Mark Bensen interjected, "Dr. Biedrzycki, what does the severity of Jessie's injuries to her neck mean to you?"

"Well," Dr. Biedrzycki said, "The severity of injury speaks to intent. It took great force to produce damage like this. And it took sustained force. This was no accident."

"And speaking of 'no accident,'" Bensen continued, "Is it true, Doctor, that if someone is choked until they lose consciousness, and if the choke hold is then released, they will revive?"

"Yes, that's true," said the doctor. "Sustained compression of the carotid arteries will cut off oxygen to the brain. At some point the person will lose consciousness due to lack of oxygen to the brain. But if the compression is released, blood flow will resume, and oxygen supply will be restored. The person will regain consciousness.

"You have to maintain compression of the carotid arteries for a significant period of time after the person loses consciousness to kill them. You have to maintain compression long enough after they pass out to stop their heart and cause cessation of brain activity."

"No further questions, Your Honor."

TELLING SEARCHES

"But you kill me through your eyes,
And your cries, and your smiles, and your lies."
—Jessie Blodgett/Ian Nytes, "Love by Proxy"

"THANK YOU, MR. BENSEN. MR. Schmaus, does the Defense have questions for the witness?"

"Yes, Your Honor."

Defense Attorney Schmaus approached the Harvard-trained Waukesha County Medical Examiner.

"Hello, Dr. Biedrzycki. Thank you for your testimony today. Dr. Biedrzycki, in all your years of practice I would imagine that you have seen many asphyxiation cases, correct?"

"Yes, I have."

"And, Doctor, I assume then that you probably have been involved in some cases of asphyxiation that were accidental, and some that were intentional, correct?"

"Yes."

"May I ask, then, if you have been involved in some cases of asphyxiation that resulted from sexual bondage games?"

There was an audible gasp from the entire left side, Jessie's side, of the courtroom. It was the bombshell defense change we had feared.

Judge Martens snapped to attention.

"The State objects to the question, Your Honor!" barked District Attorney Mark Bensen.

"Clear the jury," said the judge.

Several on the jury were visibly perturbed. They had to exit the courtroom at least a half dozen times during the trial so the judge and the two parties could discuss and debate various points outside of their presence. It was important not to prejudice them in any way.

The judge always thanked them for their patience and explained how important this part of the process was. But their patience was wearing thin. They did not appreciate prolonging their time away from work and family anymore than was necessary. And now it appeared the Defense had made some mistake that caused them to be sequestered once again. They did not seem happy about it.

We in the courtroom knew what that mistake was. Schmaus had crossed a line. In fact, he had blown right through it. It was a line the judge had clearly defined. Maybe he was desperate. The evidence was mounting, and he had nothing left but to try his ace in the hole.

"Mr. Schmaus, it was made clear before the trial started that if you were to change your defense and argue that this was an accident, then the separation of this case from the attack in the park case would be revisited, because the two cases together speak to intent. You are dangerously close to that occurring.

"I will advise you that if you persist in this line of questioning, I will be forced to reconsider my ruling. The victim in that case could be allowed to testify in this case, and evidence pertaining to that case could be heard in this one."

District Attorney Bensen argued that line had already been crossed, and that as Defense Attorney Schmaus had said himself many times during the trial, once you let the cat out of the bag, you can't put it back in. The seed had been planted in the jury's mind, whether pursued further or not.

Ali leaned over and whispered, "Melissa Richards is here and ready to testify."

But the judge was seasoned and steady, and he knew that, above all else, he must protect the integrity of this case. He would be very slow to take such drastic measures as revisiting a prior ruling and rejoining a previously severed case. The judge would err on the side of leaving no room for an appeal.

The Defense was warned. The judge recalled the jury. But my family, Jessie's friends, and especially Joy and me, were seething. The damage had been done. The suggestion had been publicly made that our daughter, who had absolutely no fault in her own murder, could have been involved in a bondage game with her killer. And that suggestion would make the Ten O'Clock News in Milwaukee. All who knew Jess well would know better. But what about the thousands of people who would see the news who didn't know her?

Jessie was the first to educate me about this common injustice in our world when she quoted Freda Adler, famous criminologist: "*Rape is the only crime where the victim becomes the accused.*"

Was that now happening to her?

It was unfair. It was despicable.

Judge Martens said, "Proceed, Mr. Schmaus."

"Thank you, Your Honor. I have no further questions for the witness."

The trial moved onward. I found myself rehearsing in my head what I would say to the press when it was all over. I would keep my vow to Jess to defend her honor and crucify Schmaus and Dan on TV, and in the papers, for having smeared her reputation. The murder I forgave, the lack of admission and apology I forgave. That miraculous forgiveness felt gifted to me from Above. It was bigger than me, beyond me, and yet it was mine to give, and mine to show everyone that it is theirs to give too.

But this I could not forgive. This was the worst evil, this lie to protect all the other lies. Her body was gone, her future was gone, her voice and her life were gone; the only thing left was her honor. And now they had attacked that, too, to save themselves.

And then I heard her voice. It wasn't an audible sound. It was inside my head. But there it was, as clear as a bell, as sweet and wise as ever, as clear as in life.

Dad, it's OK.

That was all, three words. My eyes filled with tears. The outrage melted away and the anger drained from my body. My fists un-clenched. The Great OKness filled me from my feet right up through my head and extended outward beyond the limits of my body.

Remember, Dad, you don't understand his path.

She was talking about Defense Attorney Schmaus and, of course, she was right.

My favorite Proverb fluttered into my head like a restless wind inside a newspaper box. "Reckless words pierce like a sword, but the tongue of the wise brings healing" (Proverbs 12:18). And then the next thought came: *I will crucify them.*

A strong word—crucify. It ushered into my mind the image of the cross. You know, THE Cross. And then came the next thought like a beautiful flower unfolding its petals to the sunshine after a hard rain: the whole purpose of that cross was forgiveness.

Later that day, Dana told me that Mr. Schmaus had lost a child of his own many years ago.

I saw Mr. Schmaus on a break the following day, and approached him. He saw me coming and appeared on guard. I told him I knew of his loss, and I was sorry. We shook hands and embraced briefly.

He told me he was sorry for my loss. And I saw in his eyes—those defense attorney eyes that were conditioned to seeing only contempt and judgment from people like me—the wonder that descends on someone touched by the power of Forgiveness.

"Is the State ready to call its next witness?"

"Yes, Your Honor. The State calls to the stand Ms. Ashley Boldig."

Ashley Boldig was the computer expert that helped police discover every search Dan's computer had performed. She entered from the back of the courtroom and made the long walk to the witness stand.

"She's so young. She looks nervous," Joy whispered.

Ms. Boldig appeared to be only a few years older than Jessie. How would she hold up under such pressure, especially when the defense got hold of her? But with her stylish blonde hair and conservative business suit, she had that smart look too.

I whispered back to Joy. "When it comes to computers in today's world, you want someone young!"

272

Joy and I smiled. Jess and her friends could run circles around us on the computer. And as we all found out soon enough, so could Ms. Boldig.

After the swearing-in and the usual credential formalities, the State began. Our computer expert revealed the details of what she did and how she did it. In essence, Miss Boldig had the know-how to uncover every search the computer in question had performed.

A string of famous serial killers were discovered in the history of Dan's computer, which included sub searches using keywords words pertaining to methods and the number of victims per killer. It seemed Dan wanted to know who was the best, and how they did it.

One of the serial killers—Moses Sithole—was famous in Africa for having lured dozens of women into secluded areas, then binding, sexually assaulting, and killing them, leaving them in the woods. I couldn't help but think of Richfield County Park, where Dan's first attack occurred, and where had taken Jessie for a hike just two weeks earlier.

Luis Garavito was famous in South America. He had over one hundred victims. I wondered how many victims we would have had in Washington County if Melissa Richards had not fought off Dan.

The history also showed searches for "spree killing." Following this search line, detectives found spree killing defined as "two or more victims in multiple locations over a period of at least three days." The attacks in Richfield County Park and Jessie's bedroom fit the definition to a tee.

Apparently, Dan liked the idea of being a spree killer, too.

None of this was new information to Joy and me. But then came "snuff films," films depicting women being attacked, sexually assault-ed, sometimes tortured, and ultimately killed by a man. I didn't know such films existed. I didn't know there was a subculture of men who liked to watch this genre. I didn't know Dan was part of this subculture. No one else did either.

There were multiple searches for these types of films. One occurred on the morning of July 15, 2013, before Dan raped and murdered Jessie.

I guess Dan was getting himself geared up for the big day.

This was a glimpse into the sickness infecting Dan's mind. This was a glimpse into the sickness of mankind. I briefly saw my beautiful Jess through his eyes, as a dehumanized object of titillating violent fantasy, existing purely for evil excitement, for twisted play. She was not Jessie, his friend. She was not a real person. She was just a helpless faceless sex object to torture and terrify before committing the ultimate demonstration of control—taking her life.

Dan was not alone in his fantasizing. Men watch these films every day. Many of them never act out their fantasies. Some of them do. Three women die every day in our country at the hands of a boyfriend or husband—the person in this world who is supposed to love and protect them. How was it possible for man to have wandered so far from Love? How was it possible for Love to allow this to continue?

By Tuesday of the second week, the State rested. The parade of witnesses had all testified. To my amazement, the Defense called no witnesses.

They had tried to poke holes wherever possible in the Prosecution's evidence and arguments, but those efforts appeared to have minimal success and sometimes even seemed feeble. The Defense rested, as well.

Attorney Schmaus never crossed the line a second time. There was no further innuendo, not the slightest question of accident or bondage game gone wrong. The Defense had simply tried its best to cast doubt on the testimony of the State's witnesses, but had really presented no story or explanation of its own. None.

Why did they decide not to go there? Did they think that having Melissa Richards testify would be a death blow to their defense? But why not try? It seemed doomed anyway. Was it possible that Dan would not allow his attorney to smear Jessie's name, and Schmaus just crossed the line on his own once, out of desperation, to plant whatever doubt he could in the jury's minds? Was it possible that Dan wanted the accident defense, but Schmaus wouldn't do it?

It appeared to be as cut and dried a case as one could imagine. And now, it was time for closing arguments.

chapter fifty-three

THE VERDICT

"My heart's my metronome..."

—Jessie Blodgett, "Music"

August 18, 2014

UNDER WISCONSIN LAW, THE STATE would present their closing arguments first, then the Defense would go. The State would have a chance to respond to the Defense's closing arguments and have the final word to close the trial.

D.A. Bensen delivered his statement. It was a solid, well-crafted summary of every step in the whole chain of events. He created a diagram of the main pieces of the case. He put it on the projector for all to view. Every piece of physical evidence was listed and circled, and then linked with lines. What resulted was a stunning flowchart filled to capacity with pieces of interconnected evidence. It all added up to one conclusion: guilty.

Now, it was the Defense's turn. Defense Attorney Schmaus reviewed every single piece of evidence and highlighted every tiny pocket of doubt that he had raised for each item, hoping for a cumulative effect that would add up to "reasonable doubt." It seemed to me the Defense fell so far short of reasonable doubt, though, that it only bolstered the State's case.

He just had nothing to work with. If this was a fight, the State had a loaded gun and the Defense had a slingshot. If this was a football game, the State had NFL all-stars and the Defense had college players. I don't care how good you are, you can't beat a gun with a slingshot.

Schmaus was a formidable opponent when the trial began. He was strong and believable. He had an almost mesmerizing way of making you question what seemed so black and white. He was no less professional now, but he was a warrior with a slingshot, a coach with no players.

District Attorney Mark Bensen rose for the final time, and before our very eyes he transformed. Benson became animated and emotional. His voice grew louder and louder as he talked of Jessie and the terrible loss this was.

"Jessie's body, Jessie herself, was screaming at us to solve this case!" he said, referring to Dan's DNA under her fingernails, the bruises on her elbows and knees from her futile struggling, and the deep wounds on her neck from the rope that carried the DNA of both victim and attacker.

He turned dramatically on Dan, walked toward him, pointed his finger forcefully, named him, and called him the most dangerous person he has ever seen. "He watched the snuff film, *Poor Girl Raped and Murdered*, before he attacked Jessie. It was his instructional video!" And then he called him responsible and accountable for Jessie's death.

Mark was not acting. He was as real as I have ever seen him. Our mild-mannered, courteous, and professional D.A. had let his inner father out. He had worked himself into a controlled lather and let his outrage shine. He was remembering Jess. He was remembering his own daughters. He was remembering all the daughters in Washington County that it's his job to protect. He was speaking powerfully from his own heart.

Mark might not have bowled me over with his first impression, but I will never forget his last.

Court adjourned. The case, Dan's fate, and justice for Jessie were now in the jury's hands.

As we rose from the oak bench in the front row of the left side of the courtroom, Ali, Victim/Witness Coordinator for the Washington County District Attorney's office, stopped us. Ali sat by Joy and me for the entire trial. (She made sure for a week and a half that we had everything we needed, while also making sure D.A. Mark Bensen and Assistant D.A. Sandy Giernoth had everything they needed, and that all witnesses were ready to go.)

"Stay within five minutes of the courthouse, and keep your phone on," Ali said.

No one could predict how long the jury would be out. It could be hours; it could be days. We would likely wait for the rest of the day and then have to come back tomorrow.

The jury had to review a long list of instructions. They had to elect a foreman. And they had to discuss all the points of evidence with due diligence.

My family and a few close friends went to a nearby park. We parked alongside the upper reaches of the Milwaukee River. A soft summer breeze rustled the leaves in the tall oaks and maples overhead. The rippling, rushing water gurgled below. We pulled out our coolers and settled into our foldout lawn chairs.

This was the part I hated. I mean, I loved everyone there. I should relax, enjoy nature, and enjoy the quiet time with family and friends. I've never been very good at relaxing. To do so now, while awaiting the verdict in the trial of my daughter's murder, was too much to expect of myself.

The minutes dragged like hours. We all munched on our picnic lunches and discussed all the happenings. We had our own ideas of what was to come. I think we all felt confident about the decision looming. At the same time we were nervous.

If a surprise verdict came back, if the unthinkable were to happen, it would not be the first time we were dealt a shock beyond belief. Everyone present had a real life understanding that anything can happen, and that life isn't always fair.

There's a saying that's been around in the NFL. Every old football fan knows it: *"On any given Sunday…"* It means that anything can happen in a game. It means the team that's supposed to win, the team that's favored, doesn't always win. Sometimes, the team that's supposed to win loses, and the team that's supposed to lose wins.

Fifty-four years have taught me that real life can be like sports. But at least in football you always know the score. As the game wears on, at least you always know who's winning, and how much they're winning by. In court, you don't know the score until the jury comes back with a verdict. You might feel like you're winning for the whole game, for the whole trial. But then the jury comes back and you find out you lost.

Mark and Sandy warned us you never know what the jury will do. They warned us they have seen trials where they just couldn't understand how the jury arrived at their verdict. To me and my family, the preponderance of evidence seemed clear beyond a reasonable doubt, beyond all doubt.

But then again, on any given Sunday....

So we waited.

I tried to make conversation and relax. I tried not to bite my fingernails.

Two hours and fifty minutes after we left the courthouse my phone rang. It was Ali.

"The jury is back."

"Okay, thanks. We'll be right there." I announced this to everyone.

We packed up lunch, chairs, and coolers in a flash and piled into our cars.

"That didn't take very long. Two hours and fifty minutes," I said to Joy in the van.

"That can only mean one thing," Joy replied. "I can't see them letting him off with all that evidence after such a short deliberation."

"I can't either," I said.

"All rise."

The door to Judge Martens' chambers swung open and in he came.

"Thank you. Be seated."

The door to the jury's room opened. The jury filed in one by one. Each juror found their seat. I tried to read their faces.

"Ladies and gentlemen of the jury, have you reached a verdict?"

A middle-aged man, their foreman, rose. "Yes, we have, Your Honor." He passed a folded piece of paper to the bailiff, who then walked it over to the judge.

Judge Todd Martens unfolded the paper, read silently for a few seconds, then spoke. "On the charge of first-degree intentional homicide, we the jury find the defendant...guilty."

And just like that, it was over.

I stared at Dan while the verdict was read, looking again for any reaction. I think I saw his lower lip quiver. There was no sign of surprise, or shock, or remorse. But I believe I saw fear.

Behind me, my lifelong best friend Dave shouted, "Yes!"

But in the midst of our vindication, I felt my attention being pulled to the other side of the courtroom. There sat Dan's whole family and many of his friends. Every one of them was sobbing.

I wanted to hug every single person who came for Jessie, but instead I felt pulled across the aisle to Skip, Dan's dad. His face was red, his chest was heaving with each sob. But he was looking around. His attention was not on his own pain, but on others. He was looking for who he could comfort.

He saw me coming and stood up to clasp hands and hug. I whispered in his ear, "Everyone is judging, Dan. But I'm not, and neither is God."

I hope he knew what I meant—that Dan was forgiven. Not only by me, but by God. I don't mean to offend your religious beliefs or speak as if I have any closer connection to God than you do, and you can call me crazy, but I'm not crazy. And if your religious beliefs can't harbor that a murderer could be forgiven, then they don't fully grasp Unconditional Love.

But that's OK. None of us can fully grasp Unconditional Love. I think we'll grasp it much better when we're done here, like Jess does now.

I made my way to Laura, Dan's mom. She was still sitting, surrounded by family and friends. Laura was beyond consoling, but I had to hug her anyway, tell her the same thing I said to Skip, and tell her that I thought she was a great mom. I don't know if that was the right thing to do. I don't know what I would want to hear if I was in her shoes. Probably nothing. But I had to err on the side of Love.

I couldn't imagine then, and I still can't now, the hell she must be going through every day and every night: *What did they do to my son today at Dodge County Correctional? Why did he do it? Did he really do it? Could I have done something different?*

I hope Laura knows that I meant what I said about her being a great mom, and I hope she doesn't ask herself that last question much. That last question is the wrong question. The right questions are these: Why did Dan choose to use his gift of Free Will in this way? What's in us that causes such choices? And what can we *do* about it?

Mark and Sandy invited us up to the D.A.'s office, as they always did after court. This time, my whole extended family packed into the conference room, along with the D.A.'s staff, police officers, Detective Thickens, Sergeant Clausing, and Chief Groves. It was a victory for all who had worked so hard to win justice for Jessie. Each in their own way endured great pressure for a long time. Finally, they could lay down their heavy load.

But no one celebrated. Everyone was respectful of the cloud that hung over the case, the reason we were here together. Jess was still gone.

We discussed every aspect of the case for an hour. And then, Mark did what he always did; he prepared us for what was next.

"Sentencing is in eight weeks on October fourteenth. You'll have the chance to make your statements before the court. Dan will too. He will get to go last and have the final word. Be prepared for anything."

"What do you mean?"

"Well, we've seen convicted criminals say anything and everything. Sometimes they confess and apologize."

Someone in the room said, "Dan doesn't seem ready to do that."

Mark continued, "Sometimes they continue to deny. And sometimes they even blame the victim or get combative. Who knows what he'll say?"

Finally, I asked Mark the big question. "Mark, can I talk now? I've been waiting for thirteen months. Jessie can't have her life and her future back, but can she have her voice back? It's time to launch The Project. It's time to get started on her work."

Mark looked thoughtful. For thirteen months he coached us to stay patient. He wanted no possibility of an appeal. The wheels were turning in his head. The trial was over and the verdict was in, but sentencing was still eight weeks away. Was there any potential trouble with Jessie's dad going public before sentencing?

My stomach churned. *You cannot ask me to be silent for another two months.*

Staring at the table, engrossed in thought, Mark's eyes lifted toward mine, and a slow smile broke out across his face. "I think it's okay for you to go ahead now."

chapter fifty-four

GREEN LIGHT TO LAUNCH

"So if we hate, then we should Love."

—Jessie Blodgett/Ian Nytes, "Letter to Humanity"

THE NEXT DAY THE LOVE>hate Project website went public, and so did our Facebook Page. The page had 8,400 views and 1,200 "likes" within a week. We posted the three-minute video that seemed to move people so much. Within days, 7,500 people had viewed it. People were sharing it like crazy, commenting and thanking us for our work.

The day after the verdict, I interviewed with TMJ4 and FOX6NEWS. Both interviews were top stories on the early and late evening news that night. The pieces focused on Jessie and her project, not on the drama of the case. (You can watch these news clips on our website at www.ligth.org.)

Three weeks later, TMJ4 invited me on their primetime news show *Wisconsin Tonight* as their feature story, to talk about Jessie and her legacy project. You can view this on our site too.

Not only were people interested and engaged, they were profoundly affected. They were talking, healing, and expressing gratitude for our work. I remembered back when Jess tried to talk to me about violence against women, and I worried that she would become a "man-hater" and struggle to have a healthy relationship with a life partner.

I had no idea then how right she was. I also had no idea how good she was at creating relationships, and how unfounded my worries were. It took her death for me to see that.

Her project was off to a great start.

Jess had her voice back.

chapter fifty-five

FACE TO FACE

"Find the words to make it up to me…"
—Jessie Blodgett/Ian Nytes, "Letter To Humanity"

October 14, 2014

THE STARTUP PHASE OF THE Project was an all-consuming labor of love. It gave me purpose. It gave me hope. Every minute working on it was a welcome respite from the otherwise constant sadness. Time whizzed by, and before I knew it October 14 had arrived. The Sentencing.

Joy and I saw patients in the morning, then drove separately to meet for the last time at the Washington County Courthouse. My two older brothers gave their statements first.

Dana remembered he met Dan at our vigil. "I shook your hand. It was the very hand that killed Jessie one day earlier. I wish I could take that handshake back. My brother Buck has chosen to meet this tragedy with forgiveness, for which I admire and respect him. I, on the other hand, will never forgive you for what you did to Jessie."

My brother Fred said, "He made her suffer through a brutal, terrifying, ugly death. But for me, the real tragedy of what Dan did to Jessie is worse: he robbed her of her potential. As accomplished as Jessie was for a young woman, for all the insight she had about the world, for all the richness of her friendships and bonds with family, for all her talent, she was just beginning to come into her own, just beginning to become the woman she would have been. I will never have the chance to know and love and admire and take pride in that beautiful woman.

"I have a visceral memory of Buck's phone call on July 15, 2013. His voice quivering, he told me bluntly Jessie was dead. Can you imagine that moment? I remember falling to my knees.

"I can only understand Dan's act as that of a psychopath. He inflicted this nightmare on someone who trusted him, and he did it for amusement. As cowards do, he chose an easy target. What sickens my stomach is he did it for fun.

"My family and her friends will talk about Jess forever. But most of us will choose to forget Dan. His life is meaningless now, an utter failure and waste.

"When Dan murdered Jessie, he also murdered a piece of my soul."

On the spur of the moment, my mom spoke. She shared memories of taking Jess for the day when she was a little girl, and singing together as they drove to "Gammie's house." I am proud of my brothers and my mom for their words that day.

And then it was my turn. I'd waited fifteen months for this. Most of my statement was about Jessie. But to Dan I said this:

"Dan…I forgive you, as I have every day since I learned it was you.

"I believe there is good and bad in every one of us, so I do not demonize or vilify you. That's too easy. That makes it too easy for the rest of us to separate ourselves and our humanity from you and yours. To the evil in you, that you chose to follow, I say this: This was a loss for evil and a stunning win for Love. You stole Jessie's life and future, you had power and dominion over her body for a few minutes, but never for one second did you have one ounce of power or control over her spirit, her heart, her will, her beautiful goodness, and her deep Love. Thousands came to her funeral. There has been a continuing tidal wave of love poured out from our community and beyond for a year running.

"To the good in you, I say this: you are forgiven. But you will not *know* Forgiveness, like experience it, feel it, until you tell the *truth*. The truth is the catalyst that runs the forgiveness reaction. The Truth will set you free. But only when you tell it, *all* of it, every dark and sordid detail, to yourself and the whole world.

"For four hundred and fifty-seven days you've lived a lie. You held the power to set in motion a healing process, for Joy and me, yourself, your mom and dad, and thousands who have been affected by this. You have thought only of yourself, not others. It has cost you, and us, dearly, more than you can imagine. As long as you're alive, you still have a chance to own what you did, try to make amends, and bring healing into our sick world.

"I hope you take that chance.

"As for Jess, she is now happy and free, empowered and peaceful beyond your understanding. But you are a shell of your true self. You told her before you killed her you had been making bad choices lately. May you choose well now.

"Dan, I don't think there is any way on God's green Earth that you, and others in this room, will understand or believe this, but it's true: I forgive you and I love you. Of course, I hate what you did, but that doesn't mean I can't forgive and love."

I was caught up in the moment and focused on my one and only chance to speak to Dan, so I missed what happened next. Friends in the gallery said there was another collective gasp, this time from the right side of the courtroom, Dan's side. Some sat in wide-eyed disbelief. Even the bailiff guarding the entrance choked up, friends said.

Such is the awesome power of Love Himself.

Now, to be clear, I didn't mean I loved Dan like I wanted to hang out, watch a Packers game, or go golfing. You don't have to like someone to love them. It's a statement of who and what I am, and of what I choose to bring into this world. He chose to bring violence and death into our world. I will never give hate that victory, by adding more. LOVE>hate. Martin Luther King was right: *"Hate cannot drive out hate: only Love can do that."*

What are you choosing to bring into our world? Jess found out on July 15, 2013 that no one is promised tomorrow. If all we really have is this moment, will you use it to fight for Love?

Finally, it was Dan's turn. I would like to tell you he confessed, now that the trial was over and he was found guilty. I would like to tell you he showed remorse, real emotion for Jessie, and admitted what he did. I'd like to tell you he apologized to Joy, to Jess, and everyone who loved her, and those who loved him too, for what he put them through.

But he did not. He continued living the lie.

He produced actual tears. He said he would like to give Joy and me the answers we were looking for, but he couldn't. He said one day he hoped to stand before a court that would know he was innocent.

Good luck with that one.

At one point he addressed Judge Martens and told him he didn't know whether to fear or loathe him, but he pitied him for the decision he had to make. That was a weird moment.

He also turned to his parents and declared that this had brought them all closer together. Another strange moment. They looked so ripped apart.

But I believe the truth managed to work its way out of the lie in places. For example, Dan appeared to throw his attorney under the bus when he mentioned bondage and said outright that Jessie would never have gone for anything like that.

He didn't have to say that. Call me an idiot for being appreciative for something my daughter's killer did, but I was. He made a point to clear the air, at least about that.

It made me wonder what had happened all along behind closed doors. Had Dan's attorney advised him his only chance was to claim accident, and had Dan refused out of respect for Jessie? Maybe one day I will know the answer to that, but it won't come from Dan.

Nothing he will ever say can be relied on. He has damaged his own credibility beyond repair. I find that extremely sad.

There was a second thing I appreciated. Dan and I sat ten feet apart for twenty minutes delivering our statements to each other. He looked me in the eye the whole time. Did he savagely rape and strangle Jess? Yes, he did. But in this sick and fallen world where self-gratification rules, every display of human decency is important and meaningful. At least he listened to me.

The final bit of truth that leaked out was when Dan cried real tears and said to Joy and me: "What little faith I have left that there is a Higher Power, I have because of you."

Apparently, even the person who attacked Jessie was watching her project, and was being touched by it to whatever degree he was capable of.

Judge Martens thanked all of Jessie's family for their statements. He shared closing thoughts and expressed amazement at the letters he received about what a beautiful person she was, and how the two families involved had shown kindness to one another. He complimented both parties on how they argued their cases. Then, he delivered a seething assessment of Dan's crime and his behavior since, especially his failure to use sentencing to apologize to Joy and me and admit he did it.

Then he sentenced Dan to life in prison without the possibility of parole.

chapter fifty-six

DATELINE

"Just close your eyes and leap,
You gotta land somewhere."

—Jessie Blodgett, "Overnight"

I HAD SAID NO TO *Dateline* for a year. We didn't want Jessie's story sensationalized, nor did we want to put Dan's family on national TV. But the day after the trial ended my office staff collectively said, "Are you crazy? Jessie has the right to have her story told. Her legacy project would be seen by millions. Think about what that would mean to her. Think what it could mean to victims everywhere for LOVE>hate to be seen across the country."

They were right. In the end, I weighed the pain of millions of victims of sexual violence against the pain that Dan's family might incur. I don't know if we can make a difference, but we must try. I can't let Jess down; I can't let her die for nothing. I called *Dateline*.

D.A. Mark Bensen said in his closing argument: "Jessie was screaming at us to solve this case."

I believe she was also screaming for us to solve this problem: violence against women. I recalled one of Jessie's messages from Laura Gruber: **Save the children, Dad.**

So I called Cassandra, the *Dateline* producer who attended parts of the trial. She agreed that Jessie's cause and our project were significant aspects of the story. She promised to mention LOVE>hate. They scheduled us for filming the next day.

When the episode aired, we got hundreds of emails from all over the country. *Dateline* spent their own time and money, unbeknownst to us, to make a short video about The LOVE>hate Project. They posted it on their site.

But I will always regret, for Dan's family, putting this story on national TV. The chance to prevent future attacks and bring some healing to millions of victims has to outweigh the pain of one family. But the pain of that one family must be unbearable.

On October 23, 2014 The Project had its breakout event. I presented at a school-wide assembly at Hartford Union High School. With fourteen hundred students (and their cellphones) in attendance, along with teachers, and principals from other area schools, I was a little nervous. I had been warned by professional speakers not to do assemblies.

"Good luck!" they would say, and laugh. "You need to talk to classes, not assemblies. Assemblies get a little crazy; too many kids, too much energy. They'll eat you alive."

But I knew I was supposed to talk to every kid in school, not just one troubled class. And I had Jess and the Master on my side. I asked them both to stay close. They did. I felt them. I asked them both to use me. They did. I asked them both for the words. And they came easily.

The assembly was the sweetest event I've ever done. Seven hundred young men stood and took the Real Man Pledge:

I promise…
To never ever…
Hit, hurt, or otherwise harm…
A woman, girl, or child.
I understand…
That I am bigger and stronger…
Than many women, girls, and children.
Therefore it is my DUTY…
To never hurt them…
But to always Protect, Respect, Honor, and Love them.
No matter what.

And then seven hundred young women broke out in spontaneous applause.

I told the students I was there in hopes that Jessie didn't die for nothing. According to data, one hundred of them—their friends sitting right next to them—had already suffered sexual violence. There was silence.

"Why can't they tell us?" I asked those kids. "Who are we as a culture, who are we as friends, that they can't tell us without fear of being disbelieved, judged, or blamed?"

Principal Dobner gave us the following testimonial after the assembly: *"Never in all my years as a principal have I witnessed an entire student body sit absolutely captivated for thirty-five minutes straight. This was a life-changing assembly, deeply moving and powerful. This was education at its finest. The LOVE>hate Project needs to present in every high school in America."*

Barbie Orban said: *"School counselors be ready. We had girls and young women come up to us afterward to talk for the first time. They were empowered. They were alive with new hope. They understood now they were not alone, it was not their fault, and it was time to heal. I saw victims who had lost faith in humanity transform into survivors with new strength and purpose."*

And a teacher at HUHS, Kristen Kieckhaefer, said: *"Students were transfixed…deeply moved to leave behind the distractions of texting and social media, to think beyond their own little world. They considered the plight of others, experienced radical empathy, and were inspired to become the start of a movement of lasting change."*

Five days after this assembly, The Project had its first community event: Jam the School for Jessie at HUHS. Three news stations covered it. (View the clips at www.ligth.org.)

Pastor John introduced the three speakers: Barbie, Nancy, and me. Barbie and Nancy told their survivors' stories. Afterward, three people told Pastor John they needed to talk about their own personal traumas—two more scheduled appointments for sexual violence counselling with Barbie.

Most victims of sexual violence never tell anyone. They live alone with their dark secret forever. It will haunt them, hurt them, erode their faith in humanity, ruin their faith in men, render some suicidal or depressed, kill their happiness and self-esteem, and leave them incapable of having a trusting relationship with a soul mate. One of our core messages is this: it's okay to talk about it. In fact, it's required for healing.

When you find the courage to tell your story, you will also find your freedom and power. By your example, like Barbie and Nancy, you will liberate others to find their freedom and power, too. On top of that, you will tell your attacker your Love is stronger than his hate, and you will break the code of silence that keeps this dirty little secret of families and institutions in place.

People were coming out of the woodwork to tell us their stories. Our page was getting private messages and comments. I was getting texts from students and parents I never met. It was exciting. It was validating. We were making a difference.

All the feedback made it clear. Jess was right. Her death was no isolated incident. Sexual violence happens to one in four women in our country. It's everywhere. It happens in big cities and small towns. It happens at home and at work and at church. It happens in rich families and poor. This issue was resonating very, very powerfully with many, many people. Women were just waiting for men to stand up and say "no more." And men were beginning to.

I flashed back to the tree planting, and coffee with Pastor John: *"If we were souls in Heaven, waiting in line for our next life on Earth, and if the Angel said, 'This one will only be nineteen years long, and you will die violently, but you will make a big impact and leave a legacy of change and Love. Jess would have been at the front of that line."*

Could it possibly be so?

Just a grieving dad's wishful thinking, I suppose.

A Message to Jessie

"She was the most passionate soul I ever met. I once commented that she had Atlas Shrugged *on her bookshelf, and she immediately went into a rant about how I was an "uber-Capitalist." You could talk to her for hours and feel special and wanted. She was a burning star in a world where stars are afraid to burn. She was just that kind of person who could debate, yet accept the other person's side and be open to their opinions. It was beautiful....*

We loved you and you blessed us with your love.

Wherever you are, Jessie, I hope there is plenty of hummus and tea."

—Cody Wallace

chapter fifty-seven

THE DIARY

"With this I feel free..."
—Jessie Blodgett/Ian Nytes, "Letter To Humanity"

JOY CALLED DETECTIVE THICKENS TO see if she could finally have Jessie's phone, computer, and diaries back. The sentencing was over; she wanted every bit of what remained of her girl. Thickens checked with the crime lab and got back to us a few days later. The answer was yes.

That meant everything to Joy. She needed to have Jessie's stuff. Every detail of her life, every little memory, every dumb little thing she made in grade school, all her journal entries from high school lit classes, the Sims game she so loved in which she created whole neighborhoods and families and amusement parks. And most of all her private thoughts as she grew up and struggled with teenage relationships, personal philosophies, and the meaning of her existence.

All of it was precious to Joy. She needed to read the diary and know Jessie's private thoughts in her final year.

The light of her life was taken, the core of her identity stolen with it. This was all she had left.

I came home from work a few nights later to find Joy happy and upbeat. She had visited Detective Thickens at the Hartford Police Department over her lunch break. She had Jessie's stuff.

Over the next few days Joy came to me from time to time. She shared a text she found on Jessie's phone that Jess sent to a friend the day before she left us. Or she shared a memory about watching Jess build her Sims community. Or she shared a tender moment or profound statement that Jess had penned in her diary or English Lit journal.

Sometimes, pride beamed from her eyes as she shared these things. Sometimes, she was sad beyond consoling. Sometimes she was laughing, other times empty and lost. But whatever she was, it would never stop her from picking up Jessie's phone, or diary, or English Lit notebook and looking for something, anything, to reconnect her with her daughter for a few seconds more.

I could not read Jessie's diary. I never would have tried to in life, and I wasn't sure if I should in death. I wanted to badly. But I felt like I needed to continue to respect her privacy.

I'm not sure I would have felt that way if it weren't for all the butterfly signs, the noise from above, the bangs, the music in the night, the flickering streetlamp, the exploding light bulb, the 67s, the Rs, and all the messages that said things like "cuddle me dad" and "feeling free in nature." If it weren't for those things, I would have thought Jess was dead and gone. I might have felt like she had no privacy left to respect.

But I no longer thought Jess was dead and gone. I now think she is with me all the time, everywhere. If I were to be reading her diary, she would be right there on my shoulder, like she is when I'm hurting, or when I'm doing a presentation for her project, or driving and listening to her CD, or when my head hits the pillow at night.

If I were to read her diary, she would be right there, giving me a knowing smile. She would be cool with it. But I wouldn't. I want her to understand I know she's there, and, for me, her diary is still hers. She can tell me what I missed when I join her.

One night after work, Joy came to the dining room when I was writing.

"Hon, look what I found," she said. Joy had Jessie's diary in hand.

We will not share the precious contents of Jessie's private diary with anyone, except for the final sentence. Late Sunday night, after the cast party, her final night on Earth, Jess laid down on her bed to write for the last time.

The last recorded thought my "atheist" daughter ever had, the last words my "atheist" daughter ever wrote, on July 15, 2013 at 12:56 a.m., before she was attacked and murdered the next morning, were:

God be with me.

Epilogue: The Beginning

"And maybe, just maybe, those butterflies
will fly free…fly free…fly free…"
—Jessie Blodgett, "Butterflies"

For most, this is where the story ends. Life moves on now. For us, now begins the long, lonely, quiet emptiness.

But in those times of the darkness, something deep inside whispers that the "long" is not so long. It's just a blip, really, in Eternal time. And something deep inside whispers that the "lonely" is a mirage; I am never alone. And then that something whispers to me about the "quiet," and how the music of Beyond is made richer by the empty quiet of this world.

We have received a lot of advice about moving on—none of it from people who have lost their only child, of course. We will never leave Jess in the past, abandoned at a bus stop in time, like some old *Twilight Zone* episode. We will carry her with us everywhere and always, just as she carries us, until our time comes and we pass through the veil between our worlds.

Until then, sweetie, in your words: "Fly free, Butterfly."

The Dream

"You're not done yet."

—Jessie Blodgett, "Overnight"

A dream within a dream....

In my dream, Jessie was floating up slowly, released from her physical pain and terror. Bewildered, adrift, she thought she was in a dream of her own. After all, her attack began when she was sleeping. Imagine waking to the realization that you were being bound and gagged.

Still gripped by disbelief and confusion over what had just happened, she saw expanding down toward her the warm, radiant, beautiful Light. She not only saw it she felt it. It flowed over and through her, warming her, calming her, and reassuring her with a profound Love that all was well. The Great OKness.

And then she heard the Voice. He was chuckling....

"Welcome, my little atheist. Surprise, surprise! You are with Me again. You have done a very good job so far, but you're not done yet...."

JESSIE

THANK YOU

I wish I could share the huge "like" lists and "comment" chains following every Facebook post I made about Jess in the year after her passing. With every one, my understanding of the impact she had on so many people expanded. With every one, my understanding deepened of just how strongly this story, this case, and this issue was resonating with people in our community and beyond.

I wish I could personally thank the thousands of people who dropped cash in donation jars around town and wore a blue LOVE>hate wristband. But I can't. I have no idea who they are. But they're the ones who established this scholarship program and ensured Jessie's name would live forever in Hartford.

ABOUT THE AUTHOR

Dr. Buck Blodgett founded and directs The LOVE > hate Project, his new life purpose. He also established the Chiropractic & Wellness Group, SC, and Wellness Drs. LLC. In family chiropractic practice since 1996, and married to his soul mate Dr. Joy since 1985, he was Jessie's dad for nineteen beautiful years.

Dr. Buck is a dynamic speaker with a powerful message for schools and community groups. Since Jessie's passing, he works tirelessly to educate, motivate, and inspire young minds and hearts to add Love to our world and end violence.

The LOVE > hate Project

Our Mission

To elevate awareness in the individual, the community, the nation, and the world of the frequency, the severity, and the full damaging impact of male against female violence. To cause individual, community, national, and global change, specifically the end of male against female violence.

Our Vision

To diminish all forms of violence and increase kindness, caring, empathy, and compassion in our communities and our world, for EVERYONE, with no one left out. To elevate LOVE.

The LOVE > hate Project website:

www.ligth.org

The Website Features:

The entire original twelve page *criminal complaint* in the Jessie Blodgett murder case.

The *sentencing statement* of Forgiveness and Love delivered from Jessie's dad to her murderer.

A link to *Obsession*, the *Dateline NBC episode* telling Jessie's story, and many other news coverage pieces on the "L>h In The News" page.

A link to our *Presentation Highlights clip* on the "L>h In The Schools" page.

To purchase Jessie's original CD, *Feelings in Sound*, go to the "Products" page. This album included "Butterflies," "Letter to Humanity," and many others.

Printed in Great Britain
by Amazon.co.uk, Ltd.,
Marston Gate.